What Went Wrong

What Went Wrong

Explaining
The Fall of the
Labour Government

Michael Barratt Brown, Geoff Bish, Ken Coates,
Francis Cripps, Frank Field, Tom Forester, Stuart
Holland, John Hughes, Michael Meacher,
Frances Morrell

Edited by Ken Coates

Spokesman
For the Institute for Workers' Control

First published in 1979 by Spokesman, for the Institute for Workers' Control, Bertrand Russell House, Gamble Street, Nottingham NG7 4ET

Cloth ISBN 0 85124 280 4
Paper ISBN 0 85124 281 2

This book is copyright under the Berne Convention. All rights are strictly reserved. No part of this publication may be reproduced or transmitted in any form or by any means without permission.

Copyright © Spokesman, 1979

Printed by the Russell Press Ltd., Nottingham

Contents

1. What Went Wrong?
   Ken Coates — 7

2. The Record of the 1974-9 Labour Government – The Growth and Distribution of Income and Wealth
   Michael Barratt Brown — 34

3. Neutralising the Industrial Strategy
   Tom Forester — 74

4. The Abandonment of Full Employment
   Francis Cripps and Frances Morrell — 95

5. Public Expenditure: The Retreat from Keynes
   John Hughes — 103

6. Whatever Happened to Industrial Democracy?
   Ken Coates — 124

7. How the Poor Fared
   Frank Field, MP — 137

8. Working Relations Between Government
   and Party
     Geoff Bish   163

9. Whitehall's Short Way With Democracy
     Michael Meacher, MP   170

10. Drafting the Manifesto
     Geoff Bish   187

11. Capital, Labour and the State
     Stuart Holland, MP   207

I

What Went Wrong?

Ken Coates

As it began, so it ends. The decade from 1970 to 1979 entered, and left, to the sound of Labour Governments falling: a noise which sometimes includes a certain amount of recrimination, but which never fails to offer a positively deafening volume of apologetics.

In 1970, the recrimination came from Mr Prentice, who felt that the deceased administration had not been quite socialist enough.[1] The justifications came from Mr Wilson himself, who had no sooner picked himself up from the steps of Downing Street before he immediately set about compiling 993 pages of vigorous, and by no means entirely self-effacing, instant history. He concluded this work with these words:

> "No incoming Prime Minister, if Mr Heath takes over, in living memory has taken over a stronger economic situation. I wanted to use that as we have never been able to, in the past five or six years, to use the economic situation for building on what we have done, for example in the social services, health and education and social security and housing — to accelerate what we have been doing, to intensify and develop it. Now we hand over the means to do that, to somebody else."[2]

If, in 1979, Mr Callaghan may not offer similar comfort, this is not only because he is somewhat more modest than his predecessor. The truth is, Mr Callaghan had presided over what had been fundamentally, as well as in name, a liberal-labour coalition, covering for the International Monetary Fund. He had struggled to ride out a prolonged slump, in the hope of securing re-election during the few moments whilst the world economy rose over a minor bump of upturn before plummeting again down the next precipitous switchback. Within the restricted scope afforded by its creditors, his administration had tried to act humanely, by generating artificial youth employment measures, distributing small amounts of money for inner-city rehabilitation, and a host of similar palliatives. But within the hostile world setting, the de-industrialisation of Britain continued its gathering decline, British competivity in manufacturing markets showed none of the prayed-for signs of recovery, import domination of key sectors of home trade continued. This manifest rot was not stopped by the oil boom if its effects were temporarily offset.

The result of this baleful evolution has been a different style of apologia. It sometimes seems as if, the more harmful and stupid the measures actually taken, the more fertile the explanatory imagination. This is only true *sometimes*, however. Other times are so dismal that even the muse of plausible double-talk, so dependable a standby on most front benches, takes fear and flies. Here, for instance, is the anonymous judgement of *Labour*

WHAT WENT WRONG?

Victory, the organ of the Campaign for Labour Victory, a notable group of defenders of official inaction on almost every possible front. It begins well:

> "In 1979, we faced the electorate with a leadership that was outstanding, a record of achievement that was considerable and a promise for the future we honestly felt we could perform."

But in the next breath we are told

> "there was no way the Government could avoid a big rise in unemployment and a sharp fall in living standards, at least temporarily."

Immediately afterwards, in defence of the IMF, we learn

> "the IMF crisis became inevitable because we were too slow to adjust our spending plans, which had risen by 10% in two years, when there was no growth in the national economy at all."[3]

But who was responsible for this slow adjustment? Why, who else but the same leadership which subsequently so obediently "adjusted its spending plans" when invited by the IMF? Why their delay? Could it not have been that those responsible were striving to defend their lifelong political pledges as well as their immediate electoral commitments? And did not the "considerable" achievement include "a big rise in unemployment" and all the rest of it? As for the "promise for the future", what was it but more of the same, guaranteed to generate a need for still more of the same?

The apostasy involved in this "temporary" adjustment was not something restricted to the betrayal of the ideals of Michael Foot, or the sacred memory of Aneurin Bevan, or any of the other hallowed idols of the left. It struck right at the heart of the announced doctrines of the self-styled 'revisionist' thinkers, whichever version of the complex of ideas associated with this grouping one might choose to take. Socialist Union, for instance, in what for the New Right was at one time the key text, *Twentieth Century Socialism*,[4] widely diffused by Penguin Books in 1956, had this to say:

> "Planning for economic security means, first and foremost, planning to maintain full employment.[5] Socialists can admit no compromise with this aim, no scaling it down to 'a high and stable level of employment', no playing with the idea that 'a small dose of unemployment' might be good for production. Just as the certainty of a job is the first condition of decent living, so is full employment the first condition of a socialist economy. Even if it could be proved conclusively — and all the evidence points in the opposite direction — that a revival of the fear of unemployment would increase productivity, this would be a poor bargain and a disgraceful exchange."

If this represented the 'ethical' revisionism of Allan Flanders, there was also the 'sociological' current of C.A.R. Crosland: the main statement of which went to press in the same month as did Flanders' little book, and which spells out the precise social meaning of full employment in the dry tones of an accomplished pedagogue:

> "there has been a decisive movement of power within industry itself from management to labour. This is mainly a consequence of the seller's market for labour created by full employment.
>
> The relative strength of workers and employers does not, of course, depend solely on conditions in the labour

market. It depends also on the political balance, the social climate, the degree of organisation of the two sides, and current views about the relation between wages on the one hand, and profits, employment, or the foreign balance on the other. These factors had all changed in a manner favourable to labour even before 1939. Yet the strength of the Unions was still severely limited by large-scale unemployment; and they were obviously, and knew it, the weaker of the two contenders.

The change from a buyer's to a seller's market for labour, however, by transposing at once the interests, and therefore the attitudes, of the two sides, has dramatically altered the balance of power at every level of labour relations.

At the level of the individual worker, the decisive change relates to the question of dismissal. The employee, for whom dismissal before the war was often a sentence of long-term unemployment, can now quickly find a job elsewhere; and he has lost, in consequence, his fear of the sack, and with it his docility. The employer, on the other hand, who before the war could replace a dismissed worker from a long waiting-list of applicants for jobs, may now have difficulty in finding any replacement at all; and he has acquired, in consequence, a reluctance to dismiss, and himself has become more docile. Thus the balance of advantage is reversed, and the result is a transformation of relationships at the shop-floor level.

At the level of the plant or firm, the main change lies in the altered attitude of the two sides towards their ultimate weapons of coercion — the strike and the lockout. With unemployment, the employer can often well afford to endure a strike or initiate a lockout; the odds in the contest are on his side, while the cost of a stoppage, with stocks often high and market conditions unprofitable, may be relatively minor. But with full employment, the odds are quite different, since the workers can now hold out much longer; while the cost of a stoppage in terms of profits foregone is likely, with stocks perhaps low and a lucrative market demand, to be much greater. The employers' incentive to avoid strikes has thus increased in the same measure as the workers' prospects of winning them; the implications for the balance of power are obvious."[6]

Now, it seems reasonable to assume that if full employment (which does *not*, we agree with Socialist Union, mean simply "a high and stable level of employment") signifies, as Crosland teaches, a shift of power to workpeople, both at the level of their individual engagements and contracts, and at the level of their collective capacity to control working conditions and to bargain jointly, then mass unemployment implies a contrary shift of power, away from the workpeople. In short, the decision to allow this "disgraceful exchange", as Labour's leading social-democratic spokesmen once rightly characterised it, involved a simultaneous abandonment of the basic assumptions of Labour's revisionists, a powerful setback to workers and their organisations, and a direct breach of Labour's own Election Manifestos which had promised "a fundamental shift in the balance of wealth and power" in a direction exactly contrary to that which was in fact brought about.

Of course, as Hugh Gaitskell wrote even before he took over the Labour Party leadership,

> "Our attitude to the problems of full employment has been greatly influenced by the 'Keynesian Revolution'. Indeed, one might almost say that just as the early Fabians were influenced by the Ricardian theory of rent and its development by John Stuart Mill, so their successors today have been influenced by *The General Theory of Employment*..."[7]

We have various things to say, below, about the ill-treatment meted out to Keynes by some of

Gaitskell's disciples. At this point, however, we might refer to that *General Theory*, to refresh our memories about one of Keynes' more important historical insights.

> "The ideas of economists and political philosophers" he wrote, in his concluding notes to that book, "both when they are right and when they are wrong, are more powerful than is commonly understood. Indeed the world is ruled by little else. Practical men, who believe themselves to be quite exempt from any intellectual influences, are usually the slaves of some defunct economist. Madmen in authority, who hear voices in the air, are distilling their frenzy from some academic scribbler of a few years back."[8]

This is a salutary thought to commend to those who have been busy for two and a half decades emancipating socialism from the domination of ideas. "The British socialist movement has not been doctrinaire in its philosophy" they have often written: "like the labour movement of which it formed a part, it was empirical and tolerant".[9] R.H. Tawney, who was taken up and patronised by this school of anti-ideologues, and who as a result of the villainies done in his name is now revolving in his grave at the speed of sound at least, once expressed his distaste for philosophies of history, to which, he told us, he maintained an attitude like that of a little London girl, who, when asked by her teacher to explain the use of pins, replied

> "Pins are very useful things; they have saved many people's lives by not a-swallerin' of them."[10]

This was good advice by a historian to historians. It was, however, dangerous advice to a group of politicians, even Labour ones, more particularly when some of them might climb into or sit close by the seats of power. For such men and women, Keynes' admonishments are sounder: they are otherwise all too prone to reject general ideas for the allegedly practical option, and to throw even the most elementary sense of duty or justice into the same convenient basket in which Tawney kept the philosophy of history.

The Callaghan administration was not mad, nor deliberately wicked, and if it did hear voices in the air telling it to consecrate the five-per cent norm in a cathedral in Rheims, unlike St. Joan, it readily recanted when it observed certain instruments being warmed on pyres outside Congress House. But it was composed of people who, in the main, had no time for doctrine, and who found themselves the more surprised to hear their own voices inadvertently talking in dilute versions of monetarist jargon, while the dole queues snaked up to a million-and-a-half in length.

It is difficult to see the results as anything other than disastrous for the Labour Movement, since they have done much to legitimate the greatly worse unemployment which will now pursue the electoral defeat of Mr Callaghan's team. Had the followers of Crosland and the disciples of Socialist Union held up their own banners, demanding "first and foremost" the commitment to full employment, ex social democracy would not have shrivelled to its present deformed state, which rejects 'scientific' socialism as unscientific, 'utopian' socialism as chiliastic, and its own most cherished analyses as impracticable. Such an input of scepticism would have been commendable if it could leave us with any pointer whatever to useful future action: but instead it left us only with the hardly ardent hope that if this group of tolerant and genial cynics could hang on to office, worse fates might possibly be kept at bay.

Like all such evolutions, this reduction of alleged social democracy to its opposite offers a variety of unedifying spectacles. See, there goes Mr Healey, pregnant with the whitewash bucket underneath that dirty mac, up the ladder by the barn-wall to touch up the slogans. "Four legs good, two legs better" we now read, where once it said something about squeezing until the pips squeaked.

All animals are equal, but some are more unemployed than others. If the pigs celebrated this discovery, made in the course of piecemeal social engineering, by buying a wireless, putting in the 'phone, and taking out subscriptions to *John Bull, Tit-bits* and the *Daily Mirror,* the ex social democrats have recognised it by refusing to carry into their manifesto the Labour Party's virtually unanimous decision to abolish the House of Lords, and dressing up Hugh Scanlon in its regalia, rescued from Farmer Jones' old wardrobe. We should remember this when we listen to the speeches of moderate men about the present predicament in which our outstanding leaders have landed us. As the *Observer* puts it:

> "there can be no escaping the chasm that divides Left and Right. Between the Left's advocacy of import controls, greater public expenditure, and open hostility

to the Common Market, and the Right's adherence to the mixed economy, lower direct taxation and free trade, the divide is deep.

David Marquand, Labour MP for Ashfield from 1967-77, gives this profoundly gloomy, but not easily disputed, analysis of the party's split condition in the current issue of *Encounter*: 'The gulf between socialists and social democrats is now the deepest in British politics . . .

'To pretend in this situation that socialists and social democrats are all part of the same great Movement — that Shirley Williams and Bill Rodgers and Roy Hattersley really have more in common with Tony Benn and Eric Heffer and Stanley Orme than they do with Peter Walker or Ian Gilmour or Edward Heath — is to live a lie. But it is a lie which the Labour Party has to live if it is to live at all'."[11]

David Marquand is an impeccable social democrat of the new (sublated) school, which "adheres to the mixed economy, lower direct taxation, and free trade": but where does he stand in relation to 'the union of ethics and politics' which Socialist Union propounded, on the material foundation of full employment? The argument in the beginning was that various items of socialist ideological baggage could now be dispensed with, since full employment had in fact brought about an "irreversible shift" in the balance of power. Having presided over the reversal of this irreversible event, the ex-social democrats do not send forth messengers to retrieve that which was necessary in the intellectual legacy which they left behind. Instead, they denounce as socialists, marxists or worse all those who still hanker for some part of the old understanding upon which, once, all were adamantly agreed. Those who share the commitment of

WHAT WENT WRONG?

Tawney or Crosland to ideals of social justice find themselves more firmly integrated with socialist tradition, now that experience has established the relevance of socialist prescriptions. But the minority, which already includes Reginald Prentice, Christopher Mayhew, Lord George-Brown, Lord Chalfont, and a number of other former Labour ministers, actively prefer to associate with anti-socialist parties rather than to remain involved with a genuinely Labour movement.

If the substance of the new conservatism has been the restoration of mass-unemployment, its badge has been its attitude to the (at first sight) subordinate issue of the House of Lords.

For the popular press, and for some of the Labour front bench, this has become the badge of the 'bolshevism' of Tony Benn and his colleagues. Labour Party policy on this matter is transparently clear. Here is the text of the motion moved by Jack Jones at the 1977 Conference:

> "This Conference declares that the House of Lords is a negation of democracy and calls upon the Government, the Parliamentary Party and the National Executive Committee to take every possible step open to them to secure the total abolition of the House of Lords, and the reform of Parliament into an efficient, single chamber, legislating body, without delay.
> Conference calls for this measure to be included in the next manifesto as set out in the National Executive Committee paper. Conference instructs the National Executive Committee to organise a great campaign throughout the movement on this issue."[13]

Never has a resolution been more overwhelmingly adopted: 6,248,000 votes were recorded in its favour, to 91,000 against.

The reasoned case for this commitment was argued in a statement submitted by the National Executive Committee to the same Conference:

> "Since the publication of our 1976 Programme, the House of Lords has shown by its actions that our description of it is more than justified — and the Lords have shown quite clearly that action to deal with an unrepresentative Second Chamber can no longer be delayed.
>
> The main function of the Lords is supposed to be that of a revising chamber but, as the Prime Minister has pointed out, it has taken on the role of a wrecking chamber. Most of the major pieces of legislation of the 1975/76 Session: the Aircraft and Shipbuilding Industries Bill, the Rent (Agriculture) Bill, the Education Bill, the Dockwork Regulation Bill, and the Health Services Bill — were emasculated in the Lords on Committee Stage and Third reading, so that they emerged virtually unrecognisable.
>
> While admittedly some of the amendments were just tidying-up amendments, others were very substantial indeed. For example, on the Aircraft and Shipbuilding Bill, the *Sunday Times* reported on 7th November 1976 that the Lords amendments would:
>
>> 'delete all ship-repairing, prohibit British shipbuilders from operating any ships, and delay vesting day of the aircraft industry until after the next General Election.'
>
> The House of Lords with its inbuilt Conservative majority, has always been hostile to Labour Governments, but even so the Lords are now being far more destructive than they were in the 1960s. In the period of the last Labour Government, between 1964 and 1970, the number of divisions in the Lords averaged 40 per year. However, in the 1974-75 session the Government was *defeated* in 100 Lords divisons, and in the recent 1975-76 session it was *defeated* in 120 divisions. It suffered eight defeats on the Rent (Agricultural) Bill, 11 on the Education Bill, 11 on the Race Relations Bill,

WHAT WENT WRONG?

17 on the Health Services Bill, 25 on the Aircraft and Shipbuilding Bill and 28 on the Dockwork Regulation Bill.

The fifth Marquess of Salisbury, who was a noted right-winger, has been quoted as saying with reference to the 1945-51 Labour Government:

> 'The Conservative Peers came to the conclusion that where something was in the Labour Party manifesto we would regard it as approved by the country . . .'

Yet now the Conservatives in the Lords appear not even to accept that. In our two election Manifestoes in 1974 we stated clearly that 'we shall (also) take (ports), shipbuilding, ship-repairing and marine engineering, and the aircraft industries into public ownership and control'. However, the Lords insisted on deleting ship-repairing from the Bill, despite the fact that the Bill had already had approximately 200 hours of Commons time, and that the Lords amendments had been rejected by the elected House of Commons several times.

Apparently, two general election victories are not enough to satisfy the House of Lords. They would it seems, prefer to rely on the considered judgement of such members of the Upper House as Viscount Simon:

> 'I find it difficult to believe that this suggestion for nationalisation started at the work bench. Naturally, I have no evidence and I am only expressing a view in the light of the way people think, but I cannot believe that the average workman thinks about that sort of thing at all.'

Of course, as has been said before, the House of Lords only takes on this role of 'interpreter of the People's minds' when Labour Governments are in office as opposed to the Conservatives. It is instructive to contrast the action of the House of Lords at present with their action (or lack thereof) on the EEC Bill when the last Conservative Government was in office:

> 'The Bill was brief and incomplete . . . in their anxiety to pass the Bill into law, the Government had allowed no time for Amendments, even on a drafting point'.[14]

The Conservative majority in the House of Lords duly ensured that this major piece of legislation went through unamended, without so much as a dot or comma changed, and proceeded to pass it by a majority of 393.

It is clear that, as the Prime Minister said in the House of Commons,

'. . . time after time after time there has been a conspiracy between the Conservative front bench in this House, and the inbuilt Conservative majority in the House of Lords to defeat legislation which has been passed through this House.'[15]

The Guardian pointed out on 27th October 1976 that the Government had up to then been defeated in 48 out of 49 divisions, and concluded that:

'By far the heaviest weight behind the votes on these 48 occasions, both in the moving of the amendments and the manning of the divisions lobbies, has come from the Conservative peers and those Independents who invariably support them. What is more, the insurmountable advantage which the Conservatives get from their army of hereditary members has been the main determining factor in the major votes. Four our of five of those who voted to cut the dockwork zone, four out of five who wrote the delaying power into the aircraft and shipbuilding Bills, were hereditary peers — only very few of them peers of first creation. The main reason why the Government has sustained such a string of defeats in the Lords is that the Conservatives have been able to use their superior power in the unelected Upper house to do what they do not have the strength to do in the elected Lower.'

This is clearly a situation which the Labour Party cannot allow to continue."[16]

This, then, was the imperative which was specifically disobeyed by Mr Callaghan, who went to the point of exerting a personal veto (to which, it is arguable, he was not entitled) over writing any such commitment into the 1979 election manifesto.

Now, how would the ethical social democrats have viewed this matter before the great apostasy? Let us listen to Tawney:

"Talk is nauseous without practice. Who will believe that the Labour Party means business as long as some of its stalwarts sit up and beg for social sugar-plums, like poodles in a drawing-room . . . And, if Privy Councillors make up for the part, when duty requires it, by hiring official clothes from a theatrical costume-maker, who will let them for the day at not unreasonable rates, there is nothing to shed tears over, except their discomfort. The thing, all the same, though a trifle, is insincere and undignified. Livery and an independent mind go ill together. Labour has no need to imitate an etiquette. It can make its own . . .

To kick over an idol, you must first get off your knees. To say that snobbery is inevitable in the Labour Party, because all Englishmen are snobs, is to throw up the sponge. Either the Labour Party means to end the tyranny of money, or it does not. If it does, it must not fawn on the owners and symbols of money. If there are members of it — a small minority no doubt, but one would be too many — who angle for notice in the capitalist Press; accept, or even beg for, 'honours'; are flattered by invitations from fashionable hostesses; suppose that their financial betters are endowed with intellects more dazzling and characters more sublime than those of common men; and succumb to convivial sociabilities, like Red Indians to fire-water, they have mistaken their vocation. They would be happier as footmen. It may be answered, of course, that it is sufficient to leave them to the ridicule of the world which they are so anxious to enter, and which may be trusted in time — its favourites change pretty quickly — to let them know what it thinks of them. But in the meantime, there are such places as colliery villages and cotton towns. How can followers be Ironsides if leaders are flunkies?

One cannot legislate for sycophancy; one can only expose it, and hope that one's acquaintances will expose it in oneself. The silly business of 'honours' is a different story. For Labour knighthoods and the rest of it (except when, as in the case of civil servants and municipal officers, such as mayors and town clerks, they are recognised steps in an official career) there is no excuse. Cruel boys tie tin cans to the tails of dogs; but even a mad dog does not tie a can to its own tail. Why on earth should a Labour member? He has already all the honour a man wants in the respect of his own people."[17]

Of course, in Tawney's day, patronage was the merest glint in the Prime Minister's eye. All the impassioned fireworks in this short passage were provoked by the conferment of two long-forgotten Knighthoods on Labour and Trade Union functionaries. Since then, not merely Knighthoods, but peerages themselves, have become ten-a-penny. Tawneys, unfortunately, among our social-democratic leaders, are incomparably rarer. Indeed Tawney sounds, does he not, uncommonly like a less reticent and more strident incarnation of Tony Benn? Benn, however, is a leveller or worse, Tawney is dead, and how can moderate men run the country if there is no trough in which to dip the snouts of all who merit reward and recognition?

There were 129 union-sponsored MPs in October 1974. It would be laborious to calculate how many retired trade union leaders were, at that time, sitting in the other house: but by 1979 some fairly unlikely candidates had wound up on the list of life peers, which included not only Hugh Scanlon of the AUEW and Richard Briginshaw of NATSOPA, among other scourges of the Establishment, but also Lords Allen, Collison, Cooper, Williamson, Greene and Plant from the more conventional trade union centre. Mr Wilson created 152 life peers between 1964 and 1970, and a further 79 (not counting those on his controversial resignation list, who came into Mr Callaghan's roster) since February 1974. In all, 155 peers take the Labour whip, 28 of whom are hereditary peers, and the remainder, life peers. Mr Wilson also named at least 360 Knights Bachelor between 1964 and 1970, and no less than 136 since early 1974. In two periods of office, he named 24 chairmen of nationalised industry boards. This vast mill of patronage is felt far further afield than in the trade union movement, and the social weight of an OBE is probably not what once it was. But Prime Ministerial consideration is only the summit of a mountainous apparatus of other forms of official preferment, which at its lower levels may seem to be more socially functional, and therefore in some senses more justifiable than it appears to many trade unionists when it is plainly a matter of baubles and trinkets.

Before the second world war, the TUC General Council only nominated members to one dozen government appointed committees or statutory bodies. By 1948 TUC nominees were present on 60 such bodies. In origin all of these were seen as utilitarian institutions: but in practice many of them became sinecures, and were to be preferred to the purely honorific status of "Lord" this or "Sir" that because they commonly carried either a fee or a regular income, which was a valuable supplement to the retirement pension of an outgoing General Councillor.

Robert Taylor reports that Sir John Hare, the

Minister of Agriculture during the 1950s, actually complained to the TUC "about the lack of effort being put in by union nominees serving at that time on the marketing boards". "At this time" he cites George Woodcock as commenting:

> "There was no reporting back. We never knew what they were doing. In fact they did damn all . . ."[18]

Taylor goes on to report that when Vincent Tewson, an earlier TUC General Secretary, served on the (now defunct) National Economic Planning Board for the TUC "he did not even tell Woodcock what was happening".

Such Quangos (in American: Quasi-autonomous *Non*-Governmental Organizations; in English *National* Governmental) have become more and more common, and it would not be possible for a serious representative to sleep through the sessions of at any rate the more important ones.

Nonetheless, such bodies are often less effective than they might be, because they depend largely upon patronage for their existence, and lack either the legal powers or the democratic clout to compel attention. When the Health and Safety Executive goes to work, it does dispose of certain clearly defined powers which is applied within a clearly defined set of responsibilities. This is less true when we consider the work of such bodies as the Equal Opportunities Commission, or the Commission for Racial Equality, both of which concern issues of much importance.

Ideally, representative forms of democratic alliance could be evolved to discharge such functions of these bodies as are necessary, in the context of as much legislative support as might be needed. As things are, members of such quangos do not have much muscle, mainly *because* they remain unaccountable to their wider constituencies.

In 1978 the Civil Service Department produced its second directory of paid public appointments made by ministers. This revealed that ministers currently disposed of 5,600 jobs: and it also showed that 19 quasi-autonomous governmental bodies (11 of which had been disbanded) had been taken off the previous (1976) list, whilst 25 new ones had been added.

The consolidated official lists can be tabulated as follows:

Table 1: Public Appointments in the Gift of Ministers

	Salaries	Fee-paid	Unpaid	Cost
Agriculture	107	281	1,037	£143,000
Defence	26	644	1,872	n.a.
Education	11	127	594	£185,000
Employment	76	2,456	5,661	£306,102
Environment	313	856	1,102	£509,636
Energy	148	1	73	£911,000
FCO/ODM	20	12	313	£54,738
Home	54	117	2,115	£310,000
Industry	78	14	403	£727,102
N. Ireland	30	61	148	£122,810
Prices and Consumer	26	49	989	£253,750
Scotland		422		n.a. £380,000
Social Services	140	1,949	8,700	n.a.
Trade	52	9	244	£345,264
Transport	206	–	289	£488,876
Wales	69	57	412	£175,158

Source: Official Report, June 28 and 29, 1978, reproduced on March 23rd 1979, *Financial Weekly*.

The incredible growth of State patronage with the growth of the State itself raises vast problems for the Labour Movement. The answer of socialists will, it is unnecessary to say, not follow the prescription of the Thatcher Government, which is to amputate any organ of Government that seems to move, unless it might have a military or police function which could render it worthy of preservation. On the contrary, quangos commonly represent feeble concessions to vast areas of need which positively demand not less, but more, effective social intervention. Precisely for this reason, the machinery for such intervention should be constituted as democratically as possible, and rendered as accountable as is practicable to the relevant constituencies. Otherwise the numerous matters of public policy involved will all suffer from having their spokesmen stitched into the fabric of a fundamentally unrepresentative and elitist establishment.

All this renders Tawney's simple prescription for patronage more difficult to apply: but that is no reason for forgetting:

> "If the only case for 'honours' is the practical one, it seems pretty easy to meet. Let the next party conference lay down (1) that no member of the party shall accept adornments of the kind except from a Labour government, (2) that no Labour government shall confer any 'honours' except such as are essential in order to enable it to do the job for which it was given power. Were that course adopted, a Labour government would remain free to recommend the creation of such peers and Privy Councillors as it required. But we should see less of the humiliating business of Labour members succumbing, however undesignedly, to the

blandishments of a social system which the Labour Party is pledged to do its utmost to wind up."[20]

Status is one thing. Structural unemployment is another. But the attitudes of those who follow David Marquand in seeking to divide the Labour Party between social-democrats and marxists show a strangely unhistorical view: a lack of appreciation of the morality of the great social democrats, whether in defending full employment as the priority of all priorities, or in approaching equality. Tawney's passionate calls for an end to flummery and obsequiousness were not simply objections to fancy dress and medieval badges: they were a heart-cry for the recognition of common humanity, which is always brought under attack when one man or woman is (however ritually) subordinated to another.

Patronage as a political system is now, as Tony Benn has convincingly shown,[20] a major impediment to real social reform. At a different level, the restoration of mass unemployment is a disabling condition of potentially lethal force: it heightens social tensions while dividing its victims with sometimes savage internecine conflict. Wherever mass unemployment persists, democracy is in danger. By 1979, though the Labour Party in the Country remained the Party of full employment (whether its members wore favours for Aneurin Bevan or Anthony Crosland, or indeed for neither); and though in the Country it remained also the party of democracy and against corporatism or patronage, in the tradition so clearly established by Tawney, which unites what is worthwhile in both the right and the left: at the level of Government as a whole the passes to both these crucial preserves had been abandoned without a fight.

This was the moral context in which the election was lost.

Labour's share of that poll was 36.9, a post-war record low. Worse, labour's share of the trade union vote was 50% (MORI, *New Statesman*) or 51% (ITN-ORC, *Labour Weekly*) according to which set of figures you take.

In 1974, 55% of trade union members had voted Labour, but the minority split almost equally between the Conservatives on one side and Liberals and Nationalists on the other. Now the Conservatives have won 31% of the union votes (ITN-ORC, *Labour Weekly*) or 35% (MORI, *New Statesman*), thus justifying Mrs Thatcher's claim that more trade union members than ever before would vote Conservative.

Union Members' Votes

| 1979 | Con 31 | Lab 51 | Lib 14 |
| 1974 | Con 23 | Lab 55 | Lib 16 |

Independent Television News/ORC election day polls (4,000 + interviews) as reported in *Labour Weekly*, 18.5.79.

What do these figures mean?

Certainly they mean that the Labour Government has failed to rally additional support beyond its already low level of 1974. The post-war trend is ominous.

Labour Vote and share of poll

1951	13,949,000	48.8%
1955	12,405,000	46.4%
1959	12,216,000	43.8%
1964	12,206,000	44.1%
1966	13,065,000	47.9%
1970	12,178,000	43.0%
1964 (a)	11,646,000	37.1%
(b)	11,457,000	39.2%
1979	11,510,000	36.9%

Instead of consolidating ground, Labour has been losing heavily in a key area which it once dominated almost unchallenged.

Of course, there were very good reasons why trade unionists should be disaffected. Almost one and a half million people were officially unemployed. For those who still had jobs, the Government had persisted in a disastrous pay policy which provoked not so much a trade union revolt as an upsurge of membership rebellion. This in turn produced a remarkable response from the displaced premier, in which he chided the union leaders for their inability to manage the very crisis which he himself had insisted on creating, against their most earnest entreaties, and against overwhelming votes at his own Party Conference. Those who follow Mr Callaghan's line of argument, in seeking to explain the present disaster in terms of union intransigence, should rather bend their considerable analytic and persuasive powers to the task of explaining what it was that transformed the social contracting trade union saints of 1975, 6, 7 and part of 1978 into the demonic fiends about whom we read in the *Daily Mail* of last winter.

Was it all accomplished without any human agency whatever? Maybe in coming years the explanation "witchcraft" will come to take on a plausibility which for many years it has not generally held: but in the interim, it seems reasonable to suggest that perhaps Mr Callaghan and those of his colleagues who did not offer their opposition to it, had at least a little to do with this development.

Pay policy was only a fraction of it, of course. Not only on any moderately reforming view, but on any moderately conservative perspective it had been an undistinguished Government. Not only did it run away from all its more important commitments on industrial democracy, the regeneration of a manufacturing industrial base, and the maintenance of employment: it went beyond these denials of its own programme into a hitherto unlooked for major attack on public spending, which at the instance of the IMF, opened up the prospect of the holocaust which is now to come.

In spite of these obvious truths, loud noises will soon be heard, crying for the recovery of the middle ground, the loss of which has, allegedly, installed the most committed rightist government to have held office in Britain for a century or more.

Votes by Social Class

AB – professional, middle class:

1979	Con 61	Lab 20	Lib 15
1974	Con 63	Lab 12	Lib 22

Labour up 8 per cent
Swing to Lab 5 per cent

C1 – white collar workers:

1979	Con 52	Lab 29	Lib 16
1974	Con 51	Lab 24	Lib 21

Labour up 5 per cent
Swing to Lab 2 per cent

C2 – skilled working:

1979	Con 39	Lab 42	Lib 14
1974	Con 26	Lab 49	Lib 20

Labour down 7 per cent
Swing to Con 10 per cent

DE – unskilled and poor:

1979	Con 33	Lab 51	Lib 12
1974	Con 22	Lab 57	Lib 16

Labour down 6 per cent
Swing to Con 9 per cent

ITN/ORC Poll, *Labour Weekly*.

How Britain Voted
(figures in percentages)

| | *Class* | | | *Trade Union* | |
	ABC 1	C2	DE	Member	Non-Member
% of voters	35	34	31	30	70
Con	59	40	34	35	50
Lab	22	42	51	50	33
Lib	16	15	11	12	15
Swing to Con since Oct. 1974	0	10½	9	8½	5½
Lab during 1979 campaign	–½	4	3½	–2	3½

Market and Opinion Research International Polls (6,400 + interviews) as digested in the *New Statesman,* 18.5.79, by Peter Kellner.

We should therefore take careful note of the precise nature of this lost ground: trade union ground, much of it, skilled workers, many housewives, and young people added on. When we are asked to devise policies to appeal to people in such groupings, it pays to recollect exactly who they are, and to consider what they are willing to tell us about what their actual interests are, and what real expectations they nourish.

We hope that some of the papers here assembled will throw light on what, precisely, contributed to the alienation of so many Labour supporters, and how, precisely, the promise of 1974 was first checked and then set aside.

FOOTNOTES

1. Mr Prentice's article in *Political Quarterly* (Vol.41, No.2, April-June 1970) was entitled 'Not Socialist Enough': and condemned the 'drift to the right' of a Labour Government whose members 'are constantly in contact with the "establishment". With some prescience Mr Prentice drew up an indictment "of policies which never ought to have been followed by a Labour Government":

    "The pursuit of orthodox Treasury inspired restrictions to the point where unemployment is substantially above the half-million mark.

    The rigid application of public expenditure cuts — also Treasury inspired — resulting in the postponement of the raising of the school leaving age and the re-introduction of Health Service charges.

    The surrender to anti-trade union prejudices by including the penal clauses in the White Paper on Industrial Relations.

    The failure to dissociate from US policy on Vietnam.

    The attempts to settle the Rhodesian question by means of the 'Tiger' and 'Fearless' proposals.

    The extension of immigration control to the holders of British passports.

    The failure to extend aid to developing countries to reach the moderate and practical target of 1 per cent of gross national product.

This is not an exhaustive list. I have deliberately excluded some of the wider issues, such as the Common Market, prices and incomes, and defence policy, where the controversies are more complicated. The examples I have mentioned are sufficient to remind us of the all too frequent occasions when large numbers of active Labour Party members have been profoundly disappointed by Government policies. In most of these cases the Labour Party Conference is on record in favour of resolutions contrary to the Government's decisions."

2. Harold Wilson: *The Labour Government: A Personal Record,* Penguin, 1974, p.993.
3. No.11, June 1979, p.4.
4. A collective work, this was drafted by Allan Flanders and Rita Hinden, editor of *Socialist Commentary.*
5. *Twentieth Century Socialism*, p.66. An asterisk at this point leads to a defining footnote which says:

"Full employment cannot, of course, mean zero unemployment. At any moment there will always be some workers unemployed, as they change from one job to another. What is meant is as many vacancies as there are unemployed."

6. *The Future of Socialism,* Jonathan Cape, 1956, pp.30-31.
7. Hugh Gaitskell: 'The Economic Aims of the Labour Party' in *The Political Quarterly,* Vol.XIV No.1, January-March 1953, p.10.
8. J.M. Keynes: *The General Theory of Employment, Interest and Money.* Macmillan, 1936, p.383.
9. Socialist Union: *Socialism — A New Statement of Principles* 1952, p.13.
10. R.H. Tawney: *The Radical Tradition,* Penguin Books, 1966, p.177.
11. *The Observer,* 8th July 1979.
12. *Socialism — A New Statement of Principles*, pp.38 et seq.
13. The Labour Party: *Report of 76th Annual Conference,* p.270.
14. Janet Morgan: *The House of Lords and the Labour Government,* 1967-70, p.233.
15. *Hansard* 9th November 1976, Col.211.
16. The Labour Party: *Statements to Annual Conference,* October 1977, pp.13-15.
17. R.H. Tawney: *The Attack and Other Papers,* Allen and Unwin, 1953, pp.66-68.
18. Robert Taylor: *The Fifth Estate,* Routledge, 1978.
19. Official Report, 28th and 29th June 1978: reproduced in *Financial Weekly* 23rd March, 1979.
20. Letter to *New Statesman,* 22 June 1935, reproduced in issue of 11 June, 1976.
21. See Tony Benn: *The Case for a Constitutional Premiership* IWC 1979.

II

The Growth and Distribution of Income and Wealth

Michael Barratt Brown

Slump and Slow Growth

The five years 1974 through 1978 were marked by an unprecedentedly low rate of economic growth in the post-war experience of the UK economy. Industrial output barely recovered to 1973 levels in 1978. Output per person employed in industry rose by about 2% a year to give an overall annual increase in real income of just under 1%. The distribution of that miserable increase will be considered below. It has to be seen first in the light of earlier years' experience and of the worldwide development of capitalist economies. Some evaluation must be made of the causes of such a poor performance and of the extent to which the policies of the Labour Government were to blame.

The first and most obvious factor is the extremely high rate of inflation, the reduction of which came to be regarded by the Government as a first priority. To this end home demand was reduced by cuts in public expenditure and by raised taxation with the object of curbing inflation. All the post-war experience, however, had indicated that prices rise faster when economic growth is held back than

Table 1: Economic Growth and Retail Price increases in periods of Growth and Stagnation UK 1952-1978 (all figures are average annual percentage changes for the years identified)

Years (inclusive)	Period	GNP Growth (in money terms)	Price Changes	Real Growth	Growth (or decline) per person employed
1953-66	Average	5.5	2.6	2.9	2.1
1953-55 1959-60 and 1963-4	7 Growth years	6.5	1.9	4.4	3.1
1956-58, 1961-2 and 1965-6	7 Stagnant years	4.7	3.4	1.4	1.1
1967-73	Average	10.4	6.9	3.4	3.4
1967-8 and 1972-3	4 Growth years	10.0	5.5	4.5	3.7
1969-71	3 Stagnant years	11.0	8.5	2.0	3.0
1974-78	Average	17.0	16.0	0.9	1.0
1974-5	2 Slump years	20.0	22.0	−1.5	−2.0
1976-8	3 years of slow growth	15.0	12.0	2.5	3.0

Source: *National Income and Expenditure*, Blue Books and *Economic Trends*, May 1979.

when it is encouraged. This was as true in the 1974-8 period as in earlier periods. Table 1 provides the relevant comparisons.

It is evident from the second column of figures that the rate of inflation has been rising steadily over the past 25 years, but that prices always rise faster in periods of stagnation or slump. The reason is that Government measures of deflation all raise costs and, therefore, prices through higher indirect taxes, higher interest rates, currency devaluation and under-capacity working in industry. Why then do Governments pursue such counter-productive measures?

The first answer is that Government management of aggregate demand and supply in the economy, following Keynesian prescriptions, has become progressively more difficult. On the one hand the Government has had steadily to increase its share of public spending in the national product in order to maintain full employment. Keynes supposed that a short term increase could be used to check a slump and a short term cut to correct a boom. The fact is that as employment in the mainly privately owned productive industries has declined by about 2½ million jobs between 1966 and 1975, employment in the mainly publicly owned service industries has had to be expanded by over a million jobs to sustain overall employment. As a share of the national product Government expenditure rose throughout the 1960s from just over 40% to nearly 50%. In 1975 it was raised to nearly 55%. From then on under the pressure of instructions from the International Monetary Fund and Central

INCOME AND WEALTH

Table 2: UK Public Expenditure 1968, 1971, 1975 and 1978

Shares of GNP		1968	1971	1975	1978
GNP (Factor Cost)	£m	37,790	49,571	94,095	141,292
Public Expenditure	£m	18,383	23,318	51,361	72,063
as % of GNP		48.6	47.0	54.6	51.0
Current	£m	14,280	18,337	41,357	62,293
Capital	£m	4,103	4,981	10,004	9,770
Capital % of total		28.7	27.2	24.2	13.6
Type of Expenditure as % of GNP					
Debt Service		4.7	4.2	4.2	5.3
Military		6.5	5.6	5.5	5.3
Civil Government		1.8	2.0	2.2	2.0
Goods and Services		10.1	9.6	11.1	11.6
of which Public Corporations' Capital Expenditure		4.0	3.5	3.4	3.6
Social Services		25.5	25.6	31.6	26.8
Total		48.6	47.0	54.6	51.0

Source: *National Income and Expenditure* Blue Book 1966-76, *Economic Trends*, April 1979.
Note: Social Service expenditure includes pensions, benefits, social security, education, health and all public housing expenditure, gross of rent receipts.

Bank lenders to the British Government, public expenditure was cut back by cash limits and reductions in capital spending to about 51%. Table 2 shows how the cuts affected the social services and especially their capital expenditure. The result was a steady increase in unemployment from around half a million to nearly a million and a half.

The sheer scale of Government spending — over half of the National product — creates difficulties for the Government because of the way under a capitalist market economy that it has to be financed. This cannot be done as under a centrally planned economy by simply allocating resources. The state share has to be found by transferring wealth either by taxing or borrowing from the private to the public sector. As the state share rises, more and more people become liable to income tax, the profits of the most profitable companies have to be cut into, and the rising number of public employees gives them a new bargaining power to raise their wages. The most profitable companies can afford to pay high wages, the less profitable cannot, and the State cannot pay more than the average levels of productivity allow without generating inflationary price increases. As long as productivity and growth are increasing, higher taxes for all and higher wages for the public sector are seen as being quite bearable. If, however, growth and productivity stop rising, as they did from 1974 right through to 1977, the Government's problem in a capitalist market economy becomes insuperable. Its only hope is to re-establish growth, but the Labour

Government believed it could not do this without feeding the fires of inflation.

There was some truth in this. For the other cause of failing Government power to manage the economy was the reduced ability of Governments to control the money supply and rates of interest. The revival of neo-classical theories of the Friedman Chicago School type arose less because of any proven causal connection between the money supply and rates of inflation than from the loss of state control in Britain over the banking system. Throughout the 1950s the Treasury could control the UK banking system through issuing or withholding short term bills (Treasury Bills) and long term stock. From the early 1960s onwards the London Clearing Banks steadily reduced their dependence on such lending and moved into the wider world of the Euro-dollar market. At the same time, while the deposits in London-Scottish and Northern Ireland Banks about quadrupled between 1958 and 1974, deposits in overseas and foreign banks operating from London increased 63 fold to a total more than double that of the UK banks. Table 3 shows the result.

But why does the Government need to borrow? Far from it being true, as is often suggested by Tory spokesmen, that the Labour Government continually borrowed in order to cover its current expenditure, there is no evidence of this until 1978. In all previous years there was a surplus (or a minute deficit, as in 1976) on central and local Government current account. The Public Sector Borrowing Requirement that has become a sort of bogey of the Tories has been used, as is quite normal in capitalist activity, to invest directly in new plant and equipment owned by Governmental authorities and nationalised industries or to lend to the private sector at home and overseas for investment. Moreover, with the exception of 1975 and 1976 the nationalised industries were meeting much the greater part of their investment from their own savings.

Table 3: Use of Funds by London Clearing Banks 1959, 1968 and 1974 (percentages of total)

Use of Funds	December 1959	December 1968	December 1974
Cash	8	8	4.4
Money on call	7.5	14	4.7
Treasury Bills	13	5	1
Other UK Banking and Bills	2	5.5	17.9
Liquidity Ratio	30.5	32.5	28.0
Government Stock	27	13	5.1
Advances	38.5	47	63
Special Deposits	0	2	2.2
Buildings etc.	4	5.5	1.7
Total	100	100	100

Nonetheless, it is true that any government of a capitalist economy which wishes to encourage an expansion of investment in the private sector has to borrow from those who have the funds. This is increasingly the giant trans-national companies as the main centres of capital accumulation. The banks which once acted as centres of accumulation for the capital of thousands of relatively small firms and individuals have become increasingly mere intermediaries and subject to the pressures

Table 4: Public Sector Saving, Investment and Borrowing Requirement (PSBR)
(all figures in £m at current prices) UK 1973-1978

Year	Public Authorities Saving	Investment	Deficit	Public Corporations Saving	Investment	Deficit	Net Private Lending etc.	PSBR
1973	1907	3708	−1801	1267	2170	−903	−1491	4,195
1974	1226	4452	−3226	1400	3103	−1703	−1458	6,387
1975	434	5064	−4630	1681	4933	−3252	−2604	10,486
1976	−29	5492	−5521	2864	5390	−2526	−1105	9,152
1977	1198	4979	−3781	3280	4892	−1612	−504	5,897
1978	−538	5114	−5652	3633	5114	−1483	−1253	8,388

Source: *Economic Trends*.

of the big companies and not of Governments. The result is that the Labour Government — and the Tories must follow suit — had to raise interest rates and restrict public sector capital spending at the behest of the money lenders. The result can be seen in Table 5. It meant that instead of providing nearly a half of all capital investment as it did in the mid 1960s, a Labour Government was providing less than a third.

The Balance of Payments

The second main answer to the question why the Labour Government pursued such counter-productive policies lay in the worsening problem of balancing the foreign payments account. In the past this was always a problem as soon as the economy showed any signs of growth, since growth draws in imports far in excess of exports even after the balances of services and property income are taken into account. In the first year of the Labour Government, with the prices of oil and of other imported raw materials soaring, the problem was more than usually acute, and Labour, moreover, inherited a huge deficit from the Heath Government.

This initial crisis and the terms imposed for the borrowings that had to be made from the International Monetary Fund and the European Central Banks stayed with the Labour Government throughout its term of office. If Harold Wilson had not joined with the Establishment to argue for Britain's entry into the EEC, and the referendum had gone the other way, Britain could have taken independent measures to impose import controls, refuse

INCOME AND WEALTH

Table 5: Annual Changes in Consumption and Investment and Average Interest Rates UK 1969-1978 (except for the last two columns all figures are in real terms — 1975 prices — % changes over previous year)

Year	Consumption Personal	Consumption Public	Gross Fixed Capital Formation Private Dwellings	Gross Fixed Capital Formation Private Industry etc. (incl. dwellings)	Gross Fixed Capital Formation Public	Public % of total	Average Interest Rate (MLR) %
1969	+0.5	−1.5	+3	+9.8	−6.0	43.5	8
1970	+2.5	+1.5	+3.7	+2.5	−0.5	43.5	7
1971	+2.7	+3.0	+20	+1.1	+2.5	42.1	5
1972	+6.0	+3.0	+14.5	+3.3	−1.6	38.8	9
1973	+4.5	+3.3	−9.3	+8.4	+1.2	40.5	13
1974	−2.2	+1.0	−8.9	−1.0	−0.5	42.6	11½
1975	−1.4	+6.5	+7.6	−6.2	−3.8	43.5	11¼
1976	+0.2	+3.0	−3.8	+3.4	−5.4	42.7	14¾
1977	−0.9	−1.0	−5.7	+9.7	−15.0	36.8	7
1978	+6.5	+1.7	+15.3	+8.8	−9.0	31.7	12½

Source: NIESR *Economic Review*, May 1979.

loans and embark on the first stages of a democratically planned economy with socialism as its objective. As it was, almost continuous deflation marked the five years of Labour Government. The Balance of Payments problem became in fact increasingly intractable as the years went by. Deflation only made British industry less competitive. Table 6 shows the trend.

Table 6: Balance of Payments at 1975 prices, UK 1967-78
(All figures in £billions)

Year	Economic Period	Exports of Goods	Imports of Goods	Balance of Goods	Balance after including services
1967	Growth	12.0	15.9	−3.9	−3.7
1968	Growth	13.6	17.5	−3.9	−3.4
1969	Stagnant	15.0	17.7	−2.7	−2.6
1970	Stagnant	15.6	18.7	−3.1	−2.7
1971	Stagnant	16.6	19.4	−2.8	−2.3
1972	Growth	16.6	21.6	−5.0	−4.5
1973	Growth	19.1	24.7	−5.6	−4.9
1974	Slump	20.2	24.9	−4.7	−3.6
1975	Slump	19.5	22.7	−3.2	−2.1
1976	Slow growth	21.4	24.0	−2.6	−0.8
1977	Stagnant	23.2	24.3	−1.1	+1.2
1978	Slow growth	24.0	25.6	−1.6	+0.4
1979½	Growth	24.0	27.2	−3.2	−1.2

Note: The 1979 figure is an estimate for the first six months adjusted for industrial action.
Source: *Economic Trends* 1979 Annual Supplement.

By showing the deficits (and surpluses) over the years all at 1975 prices it appears that the deficit was kept within bounds. On this basis only the first years and the last six months of the Labour Government reveal a serious problem. The whole period does, however, reveal a rising share of imports in the national product, particularly of finished manufactures, which had all to be paid for by exports. It was only the rising figure of North Sea Oil exports, reaching an annual rate of one billion pounds by the first half of 1979, that made it possible to meet the increased imports. Until the oil flowed, and having no recourse to import controls, the Government was forced to try to expand exports and reduce imports by deflation of the whole economy.

The fact is that for the year 1974-5 the balance of payments problem was really very serious. The rise in prices of oil and other materials took 6.0% from the national income. No country in the capitalist world was able to maintain its increase in living standards against such a rise but the striking fact is that this increase was so quickly absorbed and exports raised in 1976 and 1977 to meet the increased value of imports. The remedial measures, however, had disastrous effects on the home market and in view of the rectifying of the overseas deficit in 1976 it is hard to understand why the Government maintained its deflationary policies of cuts in public spending and rising taxes through the next two years. The explanation is that the current deficit in previous years had been balanced by receipts of property income from British investment overseas in excess of property income due on foreign investment in the UK, and this balance was being steadily eroded.

The figures are given in Table 8 at current prices. The first columns reveal the balance both

Table 7: Imports and Exports as a Percentage of GDP – UK 1969-78

Year	GDP £b = 100	Exports Goods	Exports Services	Imports All	Imports Fuel	Imports Food	Indust. Mats	Finished Mfg.	Services
1969	39.3 = 100	18.6	6.9	18.8	2.0	4.3	8.4	4.1	6.4
1970	43.4 = 100	18.7	7.6	18.9	2.1	4.1	8.3	4.4	6.7
1971	49.1 = 100	18.7	7.1	17.9	2.2	4.1	6.9	4.5	6.7
1972	54.9 = 100	17.7	6.9	18.6	2.2	4.0	7.1	5.3	6.4
1973	63.5 = 100	19.5	7.4	22.8	2.5	4.5	9.1	6.6	6.9
1974	73.6 = 100	22.4	8.7	29.6	6.0	4.9	11.6	7.1	8.8
1975	93.1 = 100	20.9	8.0	24.4	4.8	4.2	9.3	6.1	7.7
1976	109.1 = 100	23.3	9.0	26.6	4.7	4.1	9.2	7.8	7.0
1977	123.8 = 100	25.9	9.2	27.4	3.8	4.2	10.0	8.6	6.9
1978	140.7 = 100	25.2	8.8	26.0	3.2	4.0	9.5	9.4	6.5

Note: All figures are on a balance of payments basis.
Source: *National Institute Economic Review*.

on the Government's borrowing and lending account and the balance on the private sector's accounts. Remembering the twofold rise in prices between 1973 and 1978 the collapse of these balances from 1974 is the more serious. But this is not all.

An important item in the Balance of Payments is shown in the last columns of Table 8. This is the rising Government deficit not only on property income from borrowing and lending overseas but on transfers. These comprise grants to overseas Governments and, more important recently, the payments to the EEC less receipts from the EEC. The balance with the EEC is estimated to have risen by 1978 to £790m plus another £350m on food costs.

It will be evident from aggregating Tables 7 and 8 that there is a growing overall deficit on the Balance of Payments Current Account, which has had to be met by private capital movements or by Government borrowing and the running down of the Government's currency reserves. Table 9 shows how this has been done.

Table 9 can only be understood by recalling that historically British capital has always been able to build up a balance on current account from goods and services *and* net receipts of property income to finance investments overseas. From 1973 to 1977 there was no such balance and the net outflow of private investment was negative with the exception of 1972 until it was re-established in 1978. The massive build up of reserves in 1977 not only permitted this outflow of long term capital

Table 8: Property Income and Transfers in the Balance of Payments
(all figures in £ billions current prices)

Year	Property Income received In Govt.	Private	Property Income Due Out Govt.	Private	Balance on Property Income Govt.	Private	Balance of Transfers Govt.	Private
1967	.05	.73	.23	.37	−0.18	+0.36	−0.18	−0.04
1968	.03	.88	.27	.5	−0.24	+0.38	−0.18	−0.02
1969	.03	1.3	.37	.47	−0.34	+0.84	−0.2	−0.01
1970	.05	1.4	.32	.57	−0.27	+0.83	−0.2	−0.05
1971	.09	1.4	.3	.68	−0.21	+0.72	−0.2	−0.1
1972	.15	1.6	.3	.9	−0.15	+0.7	−0.4	−0.1
1973	.16	2.6	.37	1.2	−0.21	+1.4	−0.3	−0.1
1974	.23	2.9	.59	1.3	−0.36	+1.6	−0.4	−0.2
1975	.28	2.6	.78	1.3	−0.5	+1.3	−0.8	−0.2
1976	.25	3.6	.9	1.7	−0.65	+2.0	−0.8	−0.2
1977	.4	3.7	1.1	2.6	−0.7	+1.1	−1.1	−0.1
1978½	.8	3.6	1.2	2.5	−0.5	+1.0	−1.7	−0.3

Source: *Economic Trends*, March 1979.

Table 9: Financing the Balance of Payments — UK 1967-1978
(all figures are in £ millions current prices)

Year	Current Account Balance	Government Government Net Flow	Capital Account Flows Private Investment In UK	Capital Account Flows Private Investment Out of UK	Other Net	Total	Financed By Official Financing	Financed By Reserves	Total
1969	+463	−99	+673	−679	−4	−109	−709	−44	−743
1970	+731	−205	+835	−789	+736	+610	−1295	−125	−1420
1971	+1090	−274	+1266	−836	+1775	+2016	−1817	−1536	−3353
1972	+135	−255	+915	−1383	+54	−545	+416	+725	+1141
1973	−999	−254	+2000	−1743	+1161	+1105	—	−228	−228
1974	−3591	+368	+3052	−1118	+1146	+3373	−46	−59	−105
1975	−1843	+135	+2146	−1281	+88	+1088	−54	+709	+655
1976	−1137	−158	+4058	−2156	+642	−1102	+810	+1027	+1837
1977	+298	+580	+5521	−2167	+1882	+5716	+1113	−9588	−8475
1978	+254	−157	+2376	−3288	−1345	−2414	−1016	+2329	+1313

Note: Other Net flows are principally the result of oil exporters and other countries' movements of Sterling Reserves, Banks' borrowings outside the Sterling area, increases in net Trade Credit supplied and in 1978 an outflow of portfolio investment. A plus in the Reserves means they were run down and a minus means they were built up.
Source: NIESR *Economic Review* May 1979.

investment by companies but also for the first time ever a really large outflow of portfolio investment to the tune of nearly £1,000 millions — that is to say an outflow of individual capitalists' funds and above all institutional funds into foreign companies.

The decline of British industry can thus be directly attributed to the outflow of industrial and finance capital. Britain has become an underdeveloped economy combining slow growth and a balance of payments deficit, high rates of unemployment and a high rate of inflation — and for the same reasons that have always applied to underdeveloped economies — viz. that the wealth generated in Britain has been siphoned out to the main centres of capital accumulation, above all inside the EEC. The falling value of exports in relation to imports which created the trade deficit in 1978 (see Table 7) can be attributed to the effect of the giant transnational companies' transfer pricing policies. More than a half of UK trade now consists of movements of goods inside the companies. Imports are overvalued and exports undervalued so that profits and capital can be transferred from Britain to other countries.

The question remains as to why the giant British companies have been deserting their historic base in Britain. It is certain that their failure to invest in British plants has been a main cause of Britain's declining competitiveness and balance of payments difficulties. The reasons for this outflow of capital might be expected to be associated with high levels of corporate taxation in Britain — but these have been steadily reduced so that they fell from 16.5%

of profits in 1974 to 6.0% in 1976 and only recovered to 9.3% in 1977 and 12.8% in 1978. It is sedulously propagated in the media that the high wages trade unions can demand are the cause of these difficulties; but Table 12 reveals relative lower levels of wages in Britain than in continental Europe in 1974-5. An alternative explanation is the proneness of British workers to strike; but days lost in disputes have declined sharply except in the Public Services, as Table 9 shows. What is clear is that on a whole range of issues British workers are prepared to challenge management's prerogatives. A situation of stalemate has emerged in Britain in which workers can stop management taking certain positive action but not stop them exporting capital; and management can stop workers realising money wage increases by passing these on in higher prices, but not get them to increase output from the same machines and plant. Neither can effectively impose its will on the other and both seem set on mutual destruction. In the meantime growth at home declines because capital is siphoned overseas.

Table 10: Working Days Lost in Disputes 1968-79
(All figures in 1000s)

Year	All Industries	Mining	Metals, Engineering, Vehicles	Services (mainly public)
1968	4,719	57	3,363	438
1969	6,925	1,041	3,739	862
1970	10,908	1,092	4,540	3,409
1971	13,589	65	6,035	586
1972	23,923	10,800	6,636	1,135
1973	7,145	91	4,800	1,608

1974	14,845	5,628	5,837	2,072
1975	5,914	56	3,932	1,006
1976	3,509	78	1,977	461
1977	10,378	97	6,133	3,050
1978	9,306	181	6,066	2,131
1979¼	6,185	1	1,520	3,043

Note: 1979 – 4 months at annual rate.
Source: Department of Employment *Gazette*.

World Wide Recession

1974 saw a slowing down in the growth of world trade and 1975 an actual decline for the first time in over 20 years. Although recovery followed in the next year, those countries most dependent on international trade and most vulnerable to foreign competition could be expected to be most seriously affected. Britain was one of these. The share of UK manufactured goods in world exports had declined from over 20% to under 10% between the 1950s and 1970s, as West Germany and Japan had steadily raised their shares. Investment in new industrial plant and equipment had gone ahead faster outside Britain than inside, the giant transnational companies steadily moving funds out of the UK and into other areas.

The check to growth in 1974-5 in Britain only aggravated this process. Industrial output and employment fell in other capitalist countries as much as in Britain, but new plant and equipment elsewhere and especially in West Germany and Japan enabled these countries to increase output per person employed. Table 11 provides a comparison of West Germany with Britain. Both show sharp falls in output. Unemployment rates in West Germany fail to reveal as many migrant workers

Table 11: Economic Indicators — UK and West Germany 1972-78

Year	Industrial Output % Annual Growth UK	WG	Consumer Prices % Annual Growth UK	WG	Hourly Earnings % Annual Growth UK	WG	Manufacturing Productivity % Annual Growth UK	WG	Share of Exports % UK	WG	Unemployment Rate % UK	WG
1972	2	4	8	5	13	10	6	6	10.0	20.2	4.1	0.8
1973	7	7	8	7	10	10	6	7	9.4	22.1	2.8	0.9
1974	-4	-2	9	7	20	9	1	2	8.8	21.7	3.0	1.5
1975	-5	-6	23	6	28	11	-1	4	9.3	20.3	4.7	3.6
1976	3	7	17	4	16	7	4	7	8.8	20.5	6.3	3.6
1977	4	3	16	5	9	6	0	6	9.4	20.7	6.8	3.6
1978	4	3	8	2	15	5	1	3	9.5	20.7	6.8	3.5

Source: NIESR *Economic Review*.

Note: Share of exports relates to world exports of manufactured goods.

who went home as workers who registered their lack of employment. The great differences are in productivity increases and in the rates of inflation in consumer prices which reflect themselves also in higher increases in British money wages. With plant in the UK operating well below full capacity we have seen that unit costs and prices rose and at the same time employers had no incentive to invest in new plant. By contrast rising productivity in West Germany made industry more competitive, kept prices down and made investment in new plant more attractive. The process is cumulative: each deflation in Britain makes for further decline; each relative expansion in West Germany strengthens her economy the more. The Marxist law of unequal development was never more obvious; the failure of neoclassical equilibrium never more certain. Lower wages in Britain fail to attract investment because the market is impoverished. Meanwhile higher wages in Germany associated with higher productivity promise attractive markets.

Earnings in the iron and steel industry in 1974 and 1975 recalculated in Swiss francs by the International Metal Workers Federation show Britain at the bottom of the Table.

It is not of course in all industries that the UK is backward. Where low wages have been combined in Britain with relatively high productivity as in the coal industry, massive subsidies have been provided by European Governments to equalise costs. Such subsidies are supposedly ruled out under EEC regulations along with tariffs and import controls and other distortions of the free market. The

Table 12: Gross Hourly Wages and Net Hourly Earnings 1974 and 1975 (in Swiss francs)

Country	Gross Hourly Wages 1974	1975	Net Hourly Earnings 1974	1975
USA	16.2	19.0	21.6	26.7
Denmark	15.5	16.2	17.4	18.4
Sweden	12.6	13.5	13.5	14.4
Norway	12.2	13.9	12.8	14.6
Belgium	11.1	12.5	11.1	12.2
Luxembourg	10.7	10.8	10.2	10.3
W. Germany	10.3	10.0	13.1	12.6
N'lands	8.7	9.3	8.4	9.0
Finland	8.2	9.9	8.7	10.5
Japan	7.6	8.2	9.2	10.8
France	6.6	–	13.0	7.0
Italy	6.0	7.4	7.7	9.5
Austria	6.3	7.0	6.9	7.6
Great Britain	5.4	7.6	6.4	9.0

Source: International Metal Workers Federation.

argument that British Governments could not use import controls under EEC rules and for fear of retaliation is that much the weaker.

Table 13: Production Costs of Coal and Subsidies – EEC Countries 1977

Country	Coal costs per ton (£)	Direct Subsidy per ton (£)	Indirect Subsidy per ton (£)
UK (including open cast)	22	0.21	0.39
France	38	14.7	38.4
Germany	38	11.93	19.8
Belgium	52	24.06	58.2

Note: Indirect subsidies are monies which in the UK are covered by the Social Security System.
Source: Coal Division, UK Department of Energy, September 1978.

It is assumed in neoclassical theory and incorporated into the basic thinking of the EEC that if low productivity and high costs in one country lead to high imports, as they have in Britain, then the fall in the exchange rate will re-establish equilibrium. Import prices will rise to check imports; export prices will fall to encourage their sale. But the rise in import prices raises costs and the fall in export prices may be inadequate to compensate for such things as poor quality, delays in delivery or unreliable after-sales service. The provision of such subsidies as those revealed in Table 13 only perpetuates Britain's failing competitiveness. For subsidised German coking coal means subsidised German steel and subsidised German cars. It is the same with French farm products under the Common Agricultural Policy. Food prices are fixed at agreed CAP prices that keep French farmers in business and well above world prices. Imports from outside the EEC must bear a levy to bring their prices up to the CAP level. Food costs are that much higher and a heavy food importing country like Britain is the worst hit.

Yet, while the British economy suffered most severely in the slump of 1974-1975 and in subsequent years of retarded growth, the recession has been worldwide. The cause is not simply the rise in oil prices and the fact that the oil states new earnings were not applied to industrial investment so much as to property speculation. There had been for many years before 1973 a steady decline in the rate of profit, reported and analysed by

Glyn and Sutcliffe not only in Britain but throughout the capitalist world.

The factors involved were seen by them as a combination of rising trade union power after a long period of full employment, and growing competition between the main centres of capitalist development. This competition took the forms first of sharpening industrial competition between giant transnational companies, as barriers to international trade have been steadily reduced; and, second, of the growing challenge of German and Japanese capital to the United States hegemony of the capitalist world. Exchange rates which had been fixed in relation to the dollar and only infrequently adjusted between 1946 and 1970 floated free of the dollar and gold. The giant companies became increasingly opportunistic in their loyalty to the interests of the nation states from which they had sprung.

The five years of the Labour Government from 1974 to 1979 were marked by a massive attempt throughout the world on the part of the main centres of capital accumulation, both national and company, to restructure their capital so as to improve their profits. This meant rationalisation of their operations — cutting out of less profitable activities where competition was fiercest and concentrating on their more profitable activities. These were mainly where they had a monopoly position or where they could see the chance of sharply reducing their labour costs.

There was no doubt what the object was: it was to prepare for the next stages of the second

Table 14: World Statistics of Output and Prices — 1971-7

| Years | Annual % Changes in Output ||| Annual % Changes in Price[3] ||
	Agriculture	Industry[1]	Foreign Trade[2]	Food and Materials	Fuel	Manufactures
1971	+1	+4	+6	+2	+23	+6
1972	−3	+6.5	+8	+10	+8	+7
1973	+8	+8	+11	+30	+35	+20
1974	−1	+1.5	+3	+28	+385	+21
1975	+2	−1	−4	+1	+8	+11
1976	+1	+7.5	+12	+1.5	+10	−1
1977	+1.5	+4.5	+4	+11	+10	+9

Notes:
1. Industrial Activity figures excludes China, Korea and Vietnam.
2. Foreign Trade Figures are for Market economies only.
3. Prices of products entering world trade.

Source: UN *Statistical Yearbook 1977* and UN Monthly Bulletin of Statistics, December 1978.

Industrial Revolution. Unlike the first this will not involve the accumulation of capital only among existing centres of capital accumulation, it will require the securing of markets for establishing monopoly positions among a number of giant competitors operating throughout the world.

Income and Wealth Distribution

The Labour Government of 1974 was committed by its Manifesto and by Labour Party Conference resolutions to a major redistribution of power and wealth from the rich to the poor in the British political economy. It needs to be said that it was a commitment that few societies have ever achieved. Some have seen a shift in power from one elite to another, some have seen a check to the growth of one kind of power, but a major redistribution is a hard task. At low levels of development it is an almost impossible task because the very means of economic development imply a transfer from existing consumption into future investment. At higher levels of development as in Britain today transfers of wealth can be eased when the whole economy is growing. But a transfer of wealth that involves actual cuts in the consumption of the better-off to improve the condition of the worse-off is an almost impossible prescription. Yet, as we have seen, the period of the 1974-79 Labour Government was one of almost nil growth. Any transfers to improve the lot of the poor would have meant cuts in the living standards of the better off; and, given the tax structure, this in fact meant cuts in better paid workers' incomes as well as increased

Table 15: Income Shares as a percentage of Gross National Product at Factor Cost:
United Kingdom 1860-9 to 1976

Years	Employee Compensation	Income from Self-Employment Farmers	Income from Self-Employment Others	Corporate Profits	Rent	Total Domestic Profits	Net Property Income from Abroad	Gross National Product
1860-9	45.2	6.4		30.6	14.8		3.0	100
1870-9	45.2	4.5		32.1	13.7		4.5	100
1880-9	46.2	2.7		31.4	13.9		5.8	100
1890-9	48.0	2.4		30.8	12.5		6.2	100
1900-9	47.7	2.3		31.3	12.1		6.6	100
1910-14	47.3	2.5	13.7	17.1	11.0	28.1	8.4	100
1921-4	58.5	2.1	15.1	13.0	6.8	19.8	4.5	100
1925-9	58.1	1.3	14.8	12.5	7.5	20.0	5.8	100
1930-4	59.3	1.6	13.4	12.5	9.0	21.5	4.2	100
1935-8	58.9	1.6	11.6	15.0	8.8	23.8	4.1	100

1946-9	65.3	2.9	9.4	16.8	4.0	20.8	1.7	100
1950-4	65.3	2.8	7.8	18.0	3.9	21.9	2.1	100
1955-9	67.0	2.3	6.9	18.0	4.5	22.5	1.3	100
1960-3	67.4	2.1	6.3	17.9	5.1	23.0	1.2	100
1964-8	67.6		8.0	16.8	6.4	23.2	1.2	100
1969-73	68.9		9.0	13.2	7.6	20.8	1.3	100
1974	70.6		9.3	10.0	7.5	17.5	1.7	100
1975	73.5		8.8	9.3	7.4	16.7	1.0	100
1976	71.5		8.5	10.6	7.3	17.9	1.1	100
1977	69.7		9.4	13.0	7.5	20.5	0.4	100
1978	69.5		9.2	13.2	7.6	20.8	0.5	100

Sources: *1860-9 to 1960-3*: C.H. Feinstein, *The Distribution of National Income* (MacMillan, 1968), Table One, pp.116-7 as adapted by J. King and T. Regan. *Relative Income Shares* (MacMillan, 1976), Table One, p.19. *1964-8 and 1969-73* King and Regan, *op.cit.*, Table One, p.19. *1974-78* Derived by author from National Income and Expenditure data.

taxes on the rich. What then are the facts of income distribution under the 1974-79 Labour Government? We can begin with the share of wages and salaries in the national product compared with other incomes (Table 15).

There can be no doubt that 1975 marked a high point in the share of wages and salaries in the British National Income. Thereafter this share fell in relation not only to corporate profits but also to self-employment income. That it remained so high was the result of the fall in property income from abroad. The collapse of this last contribution to the strength of British capitalism has already been referred to earlier, but the Table reveals that the quantitative change from 1972 to 1977 was as great as that effected by the Second World War. By far the greater part of this recent change was the result, it will be recalled, of the investment of foreign oil companies in the North Sea. The conclusion must be that by 1977 British capitalism had become a client state, and no longer one of the majors in capital accumulation on a world scale. The result must have found some reflection in the internal distribution of income and wealth in the UK; and indeed the official statistics reveal this.

The figures in Table 16 show a steady decline in the share of the Top 1% in both wealth and income. The declining share of the next 9% is much less marked. It is a well known fact that, given the high marginal rates of income tax on large incomes, top people receive much of their remuneration in fringe benefits, top hat pension schemes, share

Table 16: Distribution of Personal Wealth in the UK 1913 to 1972

Percentage of Adult Population	Percentages of Total Personal Wealth					Percentage of all Personal Incomes from Property (pre tax)			Percentage of all Personal Incomes (pre tax)			
	1913	1936-8	1960	1972	1976	1960	1972	1949	1960	1972	1976
Top 1	69	56	42	28	25	60	40	12	8	6.5	5.7
Top 5	87	79	75	54	47	92	—	22	21	20	16.4
Top 10	92	88	83	67	62	99	85	35	34	27	26.2
Top 10 less Top 1	23	32	41	39	37	39	45	23	26	20.5	20.5
Top 20	—	—	—	82	79	—	—	—	—	43	42.3
Top 50	—	—	—	94	95	—	—	76	77	76.5	75.5

Notes: Population is defined as Tax Units. These may be married couples or single persons.
Personal Wealth includes dwellings but excludes pension rights.

Sources: 1913-1960 W.E. Meade, *Efficiency, Equality and the Ownership of Property*, 1964. 1972: *Royal Commission on the Distribution of Wealth and Income*, 1975. 1976: *Economic Trends* for November 1978 and *Social Trends*, 1979 edition.

options, a company house, a company car, servants and payments of children's school fees. The declining share of the Top 1% may thus be more apparent than real. What is most remarkable in the Table is the continuing 75% to 80% shares of the Top 20% in the total of personal wealth and of the Top 50% in the total of personal income. If there has been any redistribution it has taken place inside the top half of the population.

As a result of Incomes Policies there has certainly been some reduction in earnings differentials — among manual workers, between non-manual and manual, between men and women and between the public and private sector. Table 17 summarises these changes.

Table 17: Gross Weekly Earnings of Full-Time Workers: Differentials 1970-77

Workers	1970	1974	1975	1976	1977
Male Manual Workers					
Top decile % of Median	149.6	145.3	145.8	145.9	145.6
Top decile % of Bottom	230	219	216	214	212
Male Non-manual Workers					
Top decile % of Median	178.8	173.9	168.2	169.7	166.0
Top decile % of Bottom	309	293	282	282	274
Non-manual Median					
% of Manual Median	123	115	116	118	119
Women Medium % of					
Men Median					
Manual	51	55.5	59.5	62.5	64
Non-manual	52	55	59	61.5	62
Public % of Private					
Men Manual	93	97	105	102	100
Non-manual	103	102	106	110	106
Women Manual	100	106	112	108	105
Non-manual	140	132	140	137	130

Source: *Social Trends*, 1979 edition. NIESR *Economic Review*, February 1979.

The reduction of differentials is clear enough but much of this took place before 1974, with the exception of the improvement in public sector earnings which was reversed after 1975.

One of Labour's main claims has been that retirement pensions were raised in relation to average earnings; and this can certainly be demonstrated (see Table 18). The widely held view that supplementary benefit has been raised in relation

Table 18: Benefits as a percentage of Average Net Earnings under different Governments, UK 1961-77 (figures are percentages for October of each year)

Year	Pensions married couple	Supplementary Benefits married couple	with two children	Government
1961	36	35		Conservative
2	35	36		..
3	38	37		..
4	37	35		..
5	41	40		Labour
6	40	39		..
7	43	42		..
8	41	42		..
9	38	39		..
1970	38	37		Conservative
1	42	41	62	..
2	40	39	61	..
3	41	38	60	..
4	46	39	61	Labour
5	44	37	66	..
6	45	38	67	..
7	46	39	68	..

Note: Average earnings are taken as gross earnings of full-time male manual workers in industry *less* tax and national insurance contributions.
Source: *Social Trends*, 1979 edition.

to average earnings cannot be demonstrated however.

All the figures that we have been looking at in the last three Tables are pre-tax figures. It might have been expected that the Labour Government would have effected some measure of redistribution through taxation. It has been one of the main complaints against the last Labour Government that the effect of its tax policies was to increase the income tax rates and lower the thresholds at which income tax was payable. Table 19 taken from the 1979 Edition of *Social Trends* shows that the complaints were justified, particularly in the years 1975-6 and 1976-7 when wages increases were failing to keep up with rising prices.

From Chart 1 it can be seen that something was done to protect the lowest income group from the combined effects of higher taxes and inflation. They still suffered a 4% cut in their real disposable income between 1975 and 1977, while the highest group was cut by 12%. It would be wrong, however, to limit consideration of the incidence of taxes to the effects of income tax alone. All taxes, direct and indirect, as a percentage of income (including cash benefits) were raised from 32% in 1973 to 33% in 1974, and 36% in 1975, 37% in 1976, and only brought down again to 35% in 1978. The contribution of direct taxes was, moreover, held steady during this period and the national insurance contribution greatly increased (Table 20).

Given the large depreciation allowances granted to companies investing in new plant, the actual level of company taxes was very much reduced. What

Table 19: Proportion of male manual worker's earnings taken in direct tax (Great Britain, Percentages)

	1971-72	1972-3	1973-4	1974-5	1975-76	1976-77	1977-78
Percentage of earnings[1] taken in direct tax:							
Quantiles of earnings:[2]							
Highest decile	17	16	18	20	23	23	21
Upper quartile	15	14	16	17	21	21	19
Median	11	10	13	14	18	18	16
Lower quartile	7	6	9	10	15	14	12
Lowest decile	3	1	5	5	11	11	9
Income tax threshold[3] as a percentage of median earnings	64	69	59	60	50	51	55
Median earnings (£ per week)	28.1	31.3	36.6	41.8	53.2	62.1	68.2

1. Of a married man with two children, aged 4 and 6, and with no income other than his earnings from full-time employment and family support.
2. The earnings figures are derived from the New Earnings Survey (see Appendix B, Chapter 6: New Earnings Survey). They relate to April at the start of each year.
3. Taking account of the effects of earned income relief where appropriate.

Source: Board of Inland Revenue from Department of Employment data.

Chart 1: Changes in real disposable earnings of male manual workers,[1] 1970 prices

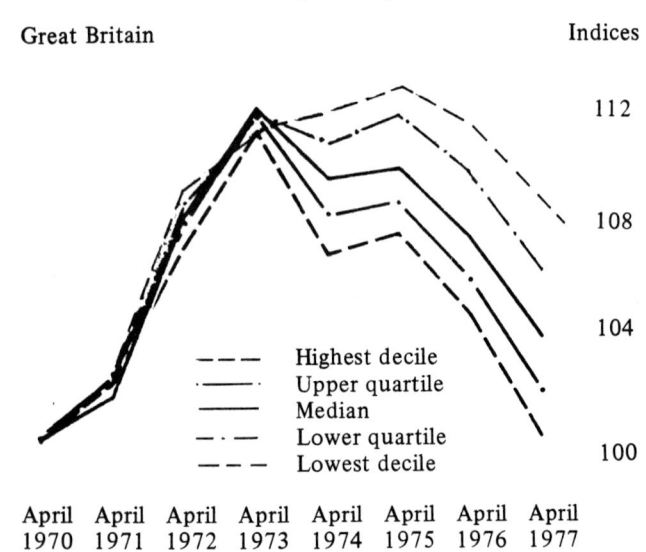

Great Britain · Indices

```
       ---   Highest decile
       ·—·   Upper quartile
       ———   Median
       —·—   Lower quartile
       ---   Lowest decile
```

April April April April April April April April
1970 1971 1972 1973 1974 1975 1976 1977

1. Married couple with two children, ages 4 and 6, whose income is the husband's earnings plus family support. Family support is the value of family allowance or child benefit, which replaced family allowances from April 1977.

Source: Central Statistics Office from New Earnings Survey data.

was reduced most radically was the contribution of indirect taxes to the exchequer. These taxes are wholly regressive in their effects and, therefore, the reduction of this source of revenue must be regarded as a very positive support for the living standards of ordinary people. At a time of rising prices any increase in indirect taxes would only have raised the rate of inflation. It was a measure of positive support by Labour that the Conservative Government was quick to correct in the first budget of the new Government in 1979. The regressive nature of the contribution of indirect taxes and national insurance deductions may be seen from Table 21. The total tax system in 1977 was linear amounting to about 37% for all income groups; but this was the result of the combination of a progressive income tax, a linear National Insurance contribution and regressive indirect taxes. Any increase in the last would be bound to make the whole tax system regressive. What the Table also shows is the balance of benefits in relation to taxes.

Table 20: Central Government Taxes and other Income by Source UK 1961-1977

(all figures, except the last lines, are percentages of total)

Source	1961	1966	1971	1975	1976	1977	1978 (est.)
Direct Taxes							
Income Tax	34.5	36.7	31.8	32.3	32.9	32.1	32.0
Corporation Tax	4.0	1.0	6.7	2.5	2.6	5.0	5.0
Taxes on Capital	3.2	2.6	3.3	1.9	1.8	1.6	1.5
Indirect Taxes	35.0	33.3	33.4	23.1	23.8	28.1	26.5
National Insurace Contributions	13.4	14.9	14.1	15.5	16.7	17.4	19.0
Other Income	7.0	7.0	6.7	3.1	7.3	7.3	7.0
Borrowing	2.9	4.5	3.2	19.0	13.4	8.2	9.0
Total	100	100	100	100	100	100	100
in £m	8.0	12.1	20.1	44.1	50.5	54.3	60.5
at 1975 prices	25.4	30.2	38.0	44.1	43.2	40.5	41.8

Source: *Social Trends* 1979 and *Economic Trends*.

Balancing the benefits and taxes, it appears that only at the two lowest deciles were families in 1977 net beneficiaries of the system and only at the highest decile could the rich be said to be making any real contribution to income re-distribu-

Table 21: UK Taxes and Benefits: Family of 2 Adults 1-4 Children 1977

Deciles	Original Income (£)	Direct Taxes	N.I.	Indirect Taxes	Total Tax	Subsidies	Cash	Kind	Net Total
1	1375	1	2	47	50	17	80	76	223
2	2923	8	3.5	25	36.5	6	11	30	120
3	3554	12	4.5	22	38.5	2.5	5	22	91
4	4043	13	4.7	20	37.7	3	3	21	89
5	4487	14.5	4.5	19	38	2	4	19.5	87.5
6	4948	14.5	4.5	18	37	2	3.5	17.5	86
7	5483	14.5	4.5	17.5	36.5	1.5	3.0	16.5	84.5
8	6110	16	4.5	16	36.5	1.5	2.5	14.5	82
9	7073	17.5	4.5	15.5	37.5	1.0	2	13	79.5
10	10827	21	3.5	12.5	37	0.5	1.5	8.5	73.5
Average	5083	15.5	4.0	18	37.5	2.0	5.5	15.5	85.5

Taxes and Benefits as % of Original Income

Source: *Economic Trends* January 1979.

tion. The great majority of the population were paying for their own benefits. Yet the problem for governments of transferring wealth from the productive sector of the economy where wealth is generated in a capitalist economy to the non-productive sector remains the main economic problem facing governments today. The problem is best illustrated by a simple model which relates

Chart 2: Productive and Non Productive Workers and Relative Productivity — a schematic model

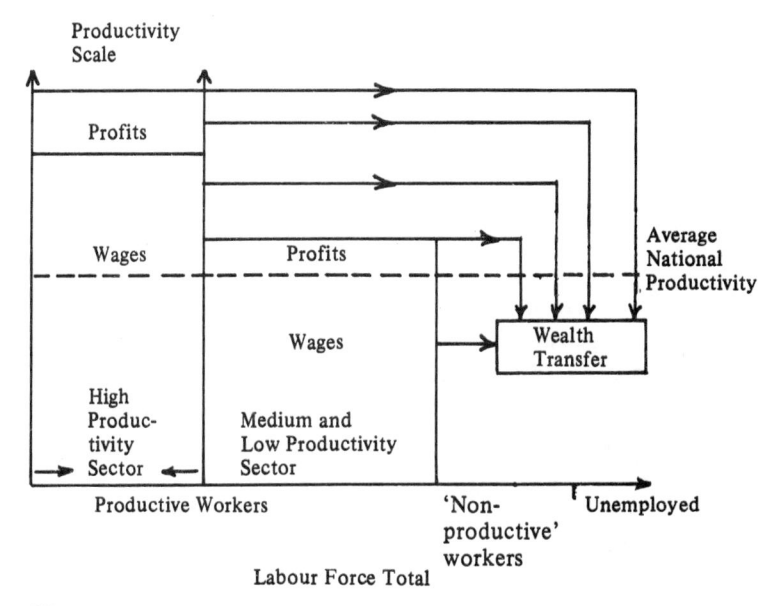

Notes:
1. Arrows in high productivity sector indicate size of workforce is shrinking.
2. Profits in medium/low productivity sector represented by block above Average National Productivity dotted line.
3. Resources for 'Non-Productive' sector come mainly from 'wages' in the productive sector and only secondarily from profits.

relative levels of productivity to various groups in the labour force.

In a market economy resources cannot be allocated directly to various sectors. Governments have to transfer wealth from the productive to the non-productive sector. Productivity can only be increased in the former which comprises mining, agriculture, manufacturing, utilities (gas, electricity, water etc.), transport and distribution. Elsewhere in the (mainly public) service sector productivity cannot be increased. But technological advance means that fewer and fewer workers are needed to produce goods and services in the productive sector. To maintain full employment governments must transfer wealth through taxation and borrowing from a smaller and smaller (mainly private) productive sector to a larger and larger (mainly public) non-productive sector. In particular, the high productivity sector employs fewer and fewer workers and steadily increases its productivity.

Transferring wealth means increasing taxes on profits and wages in the high productivity sector to maintain employment in the non-productive sector. The former declines in numbers while the latter has been growing. It is already some 35% of the labour force. The tail is increasingly having to wag the dog.

What makes the problem so unmanageable for Governments is that trade union organisation has strengthened greatly in recent years in the public sector. The result is that there is now strong pressure from public sector workers to have their wages raised up towards those of the private sector and at least (see Chart 2) up to the average national level of productivity. Once Ford workers had been granted 16% wage increases late in 1978 there was no chance of local government and hospital workers settling for 5%. As it was, the relatives between public and private sector earnings which had moved in favour of the public sector between 1970 and 1975 were reversed in the following three years (see Table 17).

The inability of capitalist institutions not only to utilise resources fully but to allocate them to meet expressed needs, may well prove to be far more serious for their survival than the falling rate of profit. The lesson of the 1974-79 Labour government is that no advantage is to be gained for ordinary people from failing to challenge these institutions at every point. What has now to be done is to create a much deeper understanding in the Labour Movement as a whole of the institutional forms that the challenge must take so that it rallies real popular power behind it.

III

Neutralising the Industrial Strategy

Tom Forester

"The crisis that we inherit when we come to power will be the occasion for fundamental change and not the excuse for postponing it". Tony Benn, rounding off the debate on Labour's new industrial policy at the Blackpool conference in 1973, caught the mood of determination among Labour Party and trade union delegates. The conference overwhelmingly endorsed a policy of vastly increased government intervention in industry with a state holding company, or "National Enterprise Board", which would take over and boost investment in profitable manufacturing concerns. There would also be planning agreements to make large companies more accountable and more responsive to the needs of the community. Government aid would in future be conditional on these agreements, which would cover investment, employment, exports, regional development, energy usage, and so on. The *Guardian* described the policy as "little short of an industrial and financial revolution".

The notion of extending public ownership and increasing state intervention in industry was no simple doctrinal imperative. The proposed system of an NEB, coupled with planning agreements, was based on study by Stuart Holland, an economist at the University of Sussex, of similar systems already operating in capitalist Italy, capitalist France and social democratic Sweden. The gist of the argument for an interventionist policy was that industry in the western nations could no longer be left to the vicissitudes of the market or the operations of the new and huge multinational companies.

The only way Italy could prevent mass emigration from the south was for the government itself to intervene and build industrial plants like Alfasud. France's post-war government laid a firm base for subsequently impressive industrial expansion by first intervening to get coal and steel properly organised and then taking controlling stakes in banks and insurance companies so that industry would not be starved of capital. In each case, a healthy industrial sector was seen as the key to all other social development − and at the same time industry was being made more responsive to social needs rather than merely private profit.

In Britain, the Conservative government had abandoned its rigorous free market "lame ducks" strategy for an ad hoc policy of unplanned subsidy to industry. Benn was later to get figures from the Department of Industry which showed that the government had given industry £3,075 million over the four years from April 1970 to March 1974. But British industry had continued to decline. Since 1970, Britain's slide down the international league table of industrial nations had not only continued, it had accelerated manufacturing capacity, share of world trade, investment per head, national output per head, relative standard of living — all the indicators pointed one way: down.

History has shown all too clearly that Labour Party programmes, evolved in Transport House and endorsed by annual conference, very often bear little or no relation to what a Labour government in Westminster will actually do. In fact, a party subcommittee had proposed a "National Investment Board" as long ago as 1931, and another study group had recommended that the state should take a controlling interest in a few large firms back in the early 1950s.

So was it likely that the next Labour government would be more likely to adopt a radical strategy, involving an extension of public ownership, than others before it?

It was — mainly because the economic crisis was deepening and Britain's weak industrial performance was all too apparent, even to the most complacent and blinkered. In the 15 years to 1973, for instance, Britain's industrial production had grown by 67 per cent, but no other European country's production had grown by less than 112 per cent. Italy's had gone up 190 per cent. Relative standards of living as measured by gross domestic product per head also showed Britain steadily dropping behind. In 1958, we were virtually on level pegging with West Germany. By 1973, their GDP per head was nearly double ours.

On the Labour Party front, Harold Wilson

INDUSTRIAL STRATEGY

himself had opened the 1973 conference debate on the new industrial policy. He set out the case for planning agreements, reinforced by new Industry Act powers, and described the NEB as a "central instrument" which would act "as a means to a further substantial expansion of public ownership through its power to take a controlling interest in relevant companies in profitable manufacturing industries". He condemned the "growing power of irresponsible domestic and multinational corporations", and argued that boardroom decisions should be made accountable. "Where public money goes, there must go a corresponding public control through public ownership".

Additionally, as Holland points out, right-wingers Roy Jenkins and Anthony Crosland had been among the first in the party to embrace the new approach. As former Gaitskellites, they welcomed the state holding company concept as a sweeter-sounding alternative to "nationalisation". An early Jenkins speech in 1972 (it reappeared in Jenkins's *What Matters Now*, Fontana, 1972) extolled the virtues of Italian state enterprise, especially the Istituto per la Ricostruzione Industriale (IRI). The speech had been drafted by Holland and was based on material contained in a collection of papers on the IRI he edited (*The State as Entrepreneur*, Weidenfeld & Nicolson, 1972). In brief, though the right was later to disown the policy, the proposals commanded broad support in their early stages. On Transport House's industrial policy subcommittee, Holland says, "the case went like a knife through butter".

However, the publication of the opposition green paper, *The National Enterprise Board: Labour's state holding company,* in April 1973 revealed that there were serious differences between Labour's social democratic wing and the left. The document, the product of a study group appointed by the industrial policy sub-committee, received extensive press coverage, largely centring on the proposed takeover of 20 to 25 large companies over about five years to give the NEB "a substantial base in the private sector . . ." and "a controlling interest over a large slice of the economy".

Harold Wilson, ever alert to the electoral embarrassment of "nationalisation" proposals, immediately let it be known that he was opposed to to the takeover and this resulted in splash headlines, like WILSON NO TO STATE GRAB. Crosland and other rightwingers on the industrial policy sub-committee tried to backtrack, but they had no alternative scheme to put forward. After a twelve-hour meeting, the party's National Executive Committee narrowly voted (by only seven votes to six) to keep the takeover commitment in *Labour's Programme 1973.* Wilson again spoke against the takeover at the October 1973 conference and, unsurprisingly, it was not specifically spelled out in the February 1974 election manifesto. More to the point, perhaps, no clear commitment was given on the size and financing of the NEB and the scale of which was being planned. Nevertheless, Labour did go into the February 1974 with a coherent and arguable case for an interventionist industrial strategy.

INDUSTRIAL STRATEGY

And the Labour government which emerged from the election did indeed "inherit" Benn's crisis. Benn took over as Secretary of State for Industry and immediately had to use the Conservative government's Industry Act to bail out a succession of failing companies. He also used the act to back new worker co-operatives at Triumph Motorcycle of Meriden, the *Scottish Daily News* and Kirkby Manufacturing and Engineering on Merseyside and to set the nationalisation of shipbuilding in motion. He began a series of talks with industry and the trade unions on the NEB and planning agreements (*The Times* commented on the early visits of trade unionists that they had "rarely been seen before crossing the portals of the DTI headquarters") and established a departmental working group under Eric Heffer, his Minister of State, to prepare a green paper on Labour's industrial strategy. Stuart Holland and Judith Hart were drafted in.

Benn further had a series of interviews with leading industrial journalists, such as Maurice Corina of *The Times,* to put the interventionist case as part of a public campaign for it. One of his main themes was the need to make industry socially accountable for the "£2 million a day" which it received in government funds — the very theme on which Wilson himself at the 1973 party conference had put such stress.

At the same time, the press took up the campaign against the industrial strategy, or "Bennery" as Whitehall now described it, and gradually its reports shifted from the industrial to the lobby writers. In the first months after February 1974, newspapers reported a public warning by Sir Michael Clapham, president of the CBI, against the "interventionist line" and noted the CBI's anxieties and "hostile stance". The crunch came with the publication in *The Times* in May of a report by Benn to the TUC-Labour Party liaison committee on progress at the DI and plans for a new Industry Act, the NEB and planning agreements. The paper envisaged planning agreements, initially with about 100 firms "controlling about half of manufacturing output", which would be agreed on a tripartite basis with the unions. These would cover "price control, the level of home and overseas sales, the regional distribution of employment, domestic investment levels, industrial relations practices and product development". The agreements were not to be compulsory, as in *Labour's Programme,* but the government's financial aid to major companies would be in-increasingly tied to agreements and their objectives. Seven targets were set for the NEB, among them a tougher bargaining stance for government with multinationals, particularly on the location of new investment, public enterprise competition against monopoly power and public control of the economy in areas of "great national interest".

The report continued "The NEB will be formed initially out of existing government holdings in industry and will then move to purchase key sector leaders in manufacturing industry". And somewhat ironically, in view of Harold Wilson's personal appointment of Sir Donald Ryder as

INDUSTRIAL STRATEGY

chairman of the NEB (an appointment Benn reputedly heard of only via his PPS), the paper argued "it will be more important that management is recruited, not via the traditional inner circuit of personal contacts, but by much more open methods".

The document, *The Times* reported, brought "bitter comments from senior [Labour] politicians who see it as electorally damaging"; and again, "Strenuous efforts are now being made by the government to halt the damaging effect of these public ownership proposals". Ministers were widely said to be seriously divided over Benn's plans, and there were equally widespread reports that he had "lost the confidence" of industry. Harold Wilson took over the chairmanship of the cabinet subcommittee to which Heffer's departmental group was to report.

Both Wilson and Denis Healey, the Chancellor, spoke publicly about the need to retain industry's confidence; Wilson said: "Private industry must have the necessary confidence to maintain and increase investment to do their duty by the people. And confidence demands that a clear frontier must be defined between what is public and what is private industry". When the draft paper came to the cabinet subcommittee, there were bitter rows from which Benn returned to the DI "utterly drained and exhausted". The white paper which emerged from this subcommittee, and then the cabinet, differed significantly from Labour's 1973 proposals and from Benn's interim report. Planning agreements were to be voluntary, and the size of the NEB was cut back; and Wilson himself wrote into the introduction a key phrase: "We need both efficient publicly owned industries, and a vigorous, alert, responsible and profitable private sector, working together with the Government in a framework which brings together the interests of all concerned".

Even so, the white paper inspired a howl of protest from industrialists, businessmen and employers' organisations, and a barrage of criticisms and warnings in the media. Labour went into the October 1974 election with a rather perfunctory mention of the NEB's role and planning agreements in the manifesto. The Industry Bill in February 1975 stuck to the watered-down version of the strategy contained in the white paper, but still drew criticism from industry. The CBI denounced it as "damaging and dangerous". Benn was by now plunging into further controversy as a leading campaigner for a "No" vote in the EEC referendum in June 1975 and anti-Benn reports in the press reached a crescendo. Most "senior and influential members of the cabinet" were widely reported to be profoundly worried by the damage he was held to be doing to confidence in the government. In May, Wilson let it be known that he would take "general direction" of the implementation of the Industry Act, and especially of the financial arrangements which also came under the control of the government.

Ray Tuite, then chief press officer at the Department of Industry, compared this period with his experience in Berlin "during the Berlin blockade".

His staff had innumerable press inquiries about Benn, even seeking confirmation of rumours about Benn's personal life and habits. "Every day it seemed there was another anti-Benn story in the papers, and we knew where they were coming from", says Tuite, with a nod in the direction of the Home Office and Treasury. "The demand for Benn to appear on radio and TV was abnormal. For a while we were getting more requests than Downing Street itself. This did not make him very popular with his cabinet colleagues. They became very jealous. Wilson in particular was worried that Benn was getting too big for his boots. With a major ministry like Industry under his control, and his links with the unions and the party, it was felt that he was building a power base to force Wilson into directions he didn't want to go".

Finally, in June, with the referendum over, Wilson was able to remove Benn from the DI. Victor Knight, political editor of the *Sunday Mirror,* who had predicted on 11 May, 1975, that Benn would be moved after 5 June, remembers Wilson calling in some lobby correspondents for a special briefing. Wilson said he was going to put a stop to "Bennery" once and for all. While the view was "made known" in political circles that continual membership of the EEC "would make Benn's position difficult", Knight points out that the equally anti-EEC Peter Shore and Michael Foot were not demoted. "Wilson told us that Benn was going too fast for his liking towards a socialist state".

A document from Labour's NEC, *Labour and*

Industry: the next steps, spelt out in October, 1975, just how the industrial legislation differed from the NEB/planning agreements strategy formerly envisaged. Planning agreements were now entirely voluntary. The government hadn't even taken reserve powers to ensure compliance after default and cash hand-outs to major companies were not tied to a planning agreement. On the NEB front, the government had failed to take powers for the compulsory purchase of companies and the funds available to the NEB (£1,000 million over an indefinite period) were inadequate since the original aim was to *double* manufacturing investment which was running at £3,000 million annually — less than half the rate per head of most industrial nations.

The NEB was so short of funds that it could do no other than become simply a repository for bankrupt "lame ducks". Tony Benn had argued for at least £1,000 million *a year,* which he regarded as the minimum necessary if the NEB were to reverse the decline in manufacturing investment in the UK (which was down nearly 25 per cent in real terms over the period 1970-76). Benn had preserved the right of the NEB to take over profitable manufacturing companies, but it didn't have the cash to do it. He had also preserved provision for information "disclosure", but this could only be triggered by the Secretary of State designating a company. (No company has been designated since the act was passed.)

Furthermore, the NEB's role since 1975 has clearly fallen short of the intentions expressed in

The watering-down of the National Enterprise Board:

Industry Act, 1975

"The functions of the board shall be:

1. Establishing, maintaining or developing, or promoting or assisting the establishment, maintenance or development of any industrial undertaking.
2. Promoting or assisting the reorganisation or development of an industry or any undertaking in an industry.
3. *Extending public ownership into profitable areas of manufacturing industry* (my emphasis).
4. Promoting industrial democracy in undertakings which the Board control.
5. Taking over publicly owned securities and other public owned property, and holding and managing securities and property which are taken over."

Official statement, NEB under Lord Ryder, March 1976

"The NEB's activities fall under the following main headings:

1. Finance for industrial investment.
2. Finance for industrial restructuring.
3. Industrial holding company role.
4. Assistance to companies in short term difficulties."

Introduction to NEB Annual Report and Accounts 1977 (May 1978) by Sir Leslie Murphy

"The NEB's *main function* is the provision of finance for industrial investment, in particular, for the expansion and modernisation of productive facilities in manufacturing industry; in addition, finance or advisory services may be provided to promote industrial restructuring. Finance is normally provided in the form of equity, but loans at commercial rates of interest may also be provided. Complementary to this function, the NEB acts as a holding company for shareholdings in industrial companies which it has acquired either through its industrial financing activities or through their having been transferred to it by the government."

the 1975 Act, which spoke for example of the NEB "extending public ownership into profitable areas of manufacturing industry" and "promoting industrial democracy". By 1978, the NEB's "main function", according to Sir Leslie Murphy, the merchant banker who now runs it, had become merely "the provision of finance for industrial investment" (see box on page 85).

In fact, the NEB has carried on three other functions. First, it has acted as an ambulance service for large "lame ducks", most notably Rolls Royce and British Leyland. This is something that governments of either colour have done anyway. Secondly, it has developed a restructuring role, sorting out firms in trouble in one particular sector (like, for instance, office equipment). This is a task formerly performed by the Industrial Reorganisation Corporation. Thirdly, and closely tied up with the ambulance function, the NEB acts as a holding company for the shares the government owns in various firms. But the board is most active in carrying out the function Sir Leslie referred to. A number of small firms, especially in sectors with growth potential like consumer electronics and computer software, have been assisted with small loans for expansion. But formerly they could have gone to other government sources or organisations, like Finance for Industry.

The point is that, worthy and laudable though the NEB's current activities are — and nobody would deny that the NEB is doing a useful job — they really have little to do with the original concept of the NEB as a dynamic body which would goad complacent firms into investing more in this country, and if they refused, would take a controlling interest in a leading firm in each sector and invest itself on society's behalf. Not only is the *kind* of activity the NEB indulges in very different, but the *scale* of the NEB's activity is also small compared with what was envisaged.

Planning agreements have fared even worse. In August 1975, Eric Varley, who replaced Tony Benn as Secretary of State for Industry, published a slim and vague document explaining what he took the term "planning agreement" to mean. In April 1976, he told Jeff Rooker MP in the Commons that he was having "operative discussions" with six companies (which he named) with a view to concluding agreements. In May 1976, he again told Rooker that three nationalised industries — British Airways, the British Steel Corporation and the National Coal Board — were entering into planning agreement discussions "over the next year".

To date, only *one* voluntary planning agreement has actually been signed — and that with Chrysler UK, who could hardly refuse because only the massive government aid given them in 1976 stopped them from going bankrupt. In 1978 they reneged on it when they sold out to Peugeot-Citroen. Ray Tuite says that planning agreements were a dead duck from the start because the CBI had made it clear that they would pull out of the National Economic Development Council (NEDC) and break off all working relations with the government if companies were forced into investment commitments.

Yet throughout the 1975-78 period, government ministers including the prime minister continued to make speeches at union annual conferences and Labour party conferences extolling the government's policy of planning agreements as a way of "getting industry moving again".

The government's so-called "industrial strategy", which was loudly trumpeted after the Chequers meeting of February 1976, was generally recognised by those in the know to be not so much a strategy, more an empty slogan.* It largely derived from a departmental draft policy paper which was presented to Benn when he first arrived at the DI. Use of the term "strategy" implied the existence of means by which agreed ends could be achieved. All the government came up with, however, were NEDC "sector working parties", which were no more than talking shops, and pious declarations, such as the NEDC's agreed "Improved Industrial Performance Scenario" of August 1976 which "provided for" a return to full employment, higher investment and productivity and a remarkable 5.5 per cent growth rate in 1977 and 1978.

Why was the interventionist strategy ditched? First, it must be remembered that in the aftermath of the three-day week the atmosphere of crisis was almost overpowering. Large firms like Ferranti and Leyland were crashing as Rolls Royce had before them. The political will for a bold policy was entirely lacking. The Labour cabinet had to choose

*See my 'What Industrial Strategy?' *Labour Weekly*, February 16 1979.

between an interventionist strategy, with an ambitious expansion of public ownership in the hands of their most militantly leftwing colleagues, and the unanimous belief of industry, big business, the Treasury and the civil service in the free market.

The ideological climate in Britain is not receptive to planning, intervention or the idea of "social" or public control of industrial or economic activities. Industry should be allowed to get on with the job of creating the nation's wealth, the argument runs. It needs to have confidence in the government's intentions if it is to invest for the future. Industrial spokesmen made plain their ideological opposition to interventionist policies and argued that their accountability was to their shareholders.

Wilson, a free marketeer and pluralist, almost certainly never believed in the strategy, and endorsed it so thoroughly at the party conference only to establish party unity for the next election. Healey, who emerged as a powerful figure in the cabinet, was always ideologically opposed to the plans which came to be seen simply as the old leftwing "nationalisation" campaign writ anew. The social democratic credo doesn't run to public control and initiative on the scale envisaged; regulation yes, rules even, and persuasion, but overall the view is that industry should be pretty well left to produce the wealth which can then be redistributed to some extent by government.

Political and personal rivalries, the row over Europe, fears about Benn's ambitions, and feelings that the Conservatives might well run off with the second 1974 election with a "nationalisation" scare, all contributed to the cabinet's decision not to back the industrial policy, particularly as the campaign in industry against "Bennery" grew in intensity and the "loss of confidence" threat was raised.

What is perhaps remarkable is the extent to which Benn's own cabinet colleagues fed the anti-Benn campaign and so sabotaged their own party's policy. The spate of unattributed "lobby" tales in the press revealed clearly what was going on. One reason was that the debate over the industrial policy became inextricably tied up with the split over EEC entry. Alex Lyon MP, who was a Minister of State at the Home Office under Roy Jenkins at the time, says that loyalty to the EEC became a "touchstone" for Jenkins and Lord Harris, the other Home Office minister. Harris, says Lyon, was doing some "very far out" things at the time. He was proposing a new centre party, for instance, an idea which received editorial support in *The Times*. Was Harris also feeding anti-Benn stories to the media? "Let's say he had close connections with Fleet Street from his journalist days. He was one of the Reform Club mafia which included people like Bill Rodgers, David Owen, and Peter Jenkins of the *Guardian*".

The civil service, too, was wholly opposed to the interventionist strategy. Adrian Ham, who was Healey's special assistant, says there was a "Whitehall-wide conspiracy to stop Benn doing anything". This conspiracy included government ministers as well as the permanent secretaries, who meet regularly in their own unofficial inner cabinet.

"Some senior civil servants went so far as to brief anti-Benn ministers behind the backs of their own ministers", he says. "They had this obsession about defeating 'Bennery' — a term coined in Whitehall long before Fleet Street picked it up". Ham says — as have others who were closely involved — that senior officials from the Department of Industry itself regularly briefed the Treasury on Benn's plans — the Treasury being the hub of opposition.

Whitehall, in fact, shared industry's free market ideology, and the DI really hankered after the more rigorous "lame duck" era. The background, education and position of top civil servants naturally lead them to identify closely with top industrialists, and many of them of course go into industry and business when they retire. Sir Antony Part, for example, who was permanent secretary at the DI during Benn's spell there, is now chairman of the Orion Insurance Company, and a director of Debenhams, EMI, the Life Association of Scotland, Lucas Industries, Metal Box and Savoy Hotels. Another former adviser adds: "They also have no real experience of industry itself, so that makes them even more willing to 'leave industry to the industrialists', the chaps who know what it's about. Interventionism is also too much like hard work, and they're ill-equipped to do it anyway".

Ham believes that many Whitehall men think that nothing can be done to halt Britain's economic decline. "There is no long term or even medium term thinking and planning is anathema to them. They even go so far as to deny that other countries like France *do* any planning". He cites the case of a Treasury brief for the Chancellor which argued that France's comprehensive system of economic planning and public ownership was really a myth. Ham, who had spent three years in Paris working for OECD and knew better, looked into the origins of the briefing paper only to find that British embassy officials in Paris had already criticised it extensively. They had produced their own more detailed document which made it crystal clear that public ownership and interventionism in the form of investment aid tied to planning agreements was much more extensive in France and had been for years. They also implied strongly that this type of industrial strategy might go a long way toward explaining France's remarkable and little-publicised post-war economic revival (industrial production grew 134 per cent between 1958-73, compared with the UK's 67 per cent).

Civil servants also show more loyalty to their superiors in the service — and to the Treasury — than to the ministers who tend to come and go. Ham says he remembers hearing one senior Treasury man telling a lower one: "Try and please the Chancellor, but remember your promotion comes from us".

Thus, from Benn's first day at the department, he was up against official hostility. Part is said to have greeted him with the following words: "I presume, Secretary of State, that you don't intend to implement the industrial strategy in *Labour's Programme*". Part, however, denies that senior civil servants undermined the strategy or Benn's own position, though he agrees that the proposals were fought hard. Benn was removed by Wilson, he told me, for reasons to do with "the cohesion and unity of the cabinet and party". It was a political decision with which the department had nothing to do (though leaks from the DI had contributed to the process of reducing confidence in Benn).

The NEB – with planning agreements – approach simply *had* to be modified, he says, "because of intense hostility from industry". Planning agreements also got confused with the industrial democracy campaign – and this scared industry which preferred a gradual "bottom upwards" approach to this kind of thing rather than the "top downwards" method. Anyway, "planning is no cure-all. Detailed plans easily become discredited". Of the twin problems of unemployment and inflation, Part says that inflation is worse: "Unemployment is a disagreeable thing, but owing to social security etc., a higher level of unemployment is more tolerable now. Firms could employ more people if the rate of growth were higher. The lack of an adequate rate of return on investment is the problem".

So where are we now? After another five years of miserable economic decline, I believe that Labour's original policy of direct state initiative is every bit as relevant today as it was in 1973. Nothing has happened to suggest that the private sector can be relied upon to act in accordance with social needs and the national good. Investment has not picked up, despite Harold Wilson's restoration of "business confidence" by sacking Benn, emasculating the NEB and Jim Callaghan's back-pedalling on planning agreements. Moreoever, the collapse of British industry in the last two years has accelerated: whole sectors like consumer electronics and consumer durables have been nearly wiped out, like motorcycles before them.*

The need to change course is urgent, yet there is hardly any public discussion of possible alternatives. Even if one disagreed with the NEB/planning agreement approach, it was at least worthy of serious consideration. One of the tragedies of this saga is that it seems to have been dismissed out-of-hand as "Bennery", or some kind of weird ideological dogma, irrespective of the fact that similar and essentially pragmatic techniques have been used widely elsewhere, especially in Europe.

Meanwhile, in terms of industrial policy, we were back where we had been during the previous Labour government. If individual firms on the verge of collapse were big enough — like Ferranti, Leyland and Rolls Royce — they got bailed out because the consequences of them going out of business altogether were too horrendous to contemplate. But less spectacular collapses and failures, or the more usual and unspectacular steady decline in performance, were allowed to go unchecked. Not only had Labour's approach to industry almost come full circle, there was very little to choose between it and the policy operated in the Heath administration of 1970-74.

*See my 'Collapse of British Industry', *Labour Weekly*, February 9, 1979. We should like to acknowledge our gratitude to *New Society*, in which a preliminary shorter draft of this article first appeared on 6 July, 1978.

IV

The Abandonment of Full Employment

Francis Cripps and Frances Morrell

When Labour took office in February 1974, unemployment stood at half a million. When Labour left office in March 1979 unemployment was 1¼ million and was expected to rise to 2 million within two or three years. The Manifesto on which Labour lost the 1979 General Election pointedly excluded any commitment to reverse this trend. Why was this?

The Labour Cabinet argued that they were forced to abandon full employment because of international circumstances beyond their control. We believe that high unemployment was a foreseeable and foreseen outcome of the policies they stood for and that they consciously chose to implement those policies instead of others which could have sustained full employment.

The choices the Parliamentary leadership made during the recurrent crises of 1974-9 showed that their primary political purpose was to protect the power of banking and multinational management and the international arrangements which supported them. If unemployment was the price they were prepared to pay it.

The End of the Historic Compromise

Following Crosland, Labour leaders had for years believed that they had the formula for full employment — namely high spending (public or private) within Britian combined with devaluation to promote exports and prevent imports, and incomes policy to control inflation. Labour's contribution consisted of choosing high *public* spending and *redistributive* taxation within that formula.

Politically, as social democrats, they stood for the existing distribution of power between the government, nationalised industries, multinationals, smaller companies and trade unions. They believed that the maintenance of the post-war settlements between these powers, which they called the "mixed economy" was an intrinsically important objective — in opposition to the socialist objective which envisaged a steady increase in common ownership under workers' control. Social democrats and socialists who upheld diametrically opposed political objectives were able to compromise and work together on the basis of the formula for full employment and high public spending.

When Labour took office in 1974 it became obvious that the formula would not work. Years of under-investment by corporate management had left British industry and its workers at a colossal disadvantage in relation to Europe, US and Japanese competition. Our industry was slowly collapsing as imports flooded into the country. Devaluation was much too weak a measure to correct a problem on this scale. As a result, exces-

FULL EMPLOYMENT

sive imports now had to be controlled by other means for which the old formula made no provision. The social democrats had to abandon either their support for the mixed economy or their support for full employment. The Cabinet decided to abandon full employment.

The Government's Options

The Cabinet's decisions during the first eighteen months of its life on the connected problems of the management of the balance of payments, wages policy, industrial policy and Britain's membership of the Common Market defined its political identity very clearly.

Ministers had a choice of two strategic positions, one free market, the other interventionist.

They could support British membership of the EEC under the Treaty of Rome: this meant dropping Labour's re-industrialisation programme as set out in the Manifesto, rejecting import controls and consequently controlling imports by cutting public expenditure to create unemployment.

Alternatively Ministers could have sought to renegotiate either the terms of the Treaty of Rome, or to challenge its total applicability to the UK as France successfully had over majority voting, or advise withdrawal. They would then have been free to implement Labour's re-industrialisation programme, control excess imports by trade agreements, and maintain full employment.

The free market position was naturally favoured by the City and multinational management since controls on the movement of capital and goods impeded international financial transactions and limited management's global freedom to decide on the location of investment. In addition the shift of power to the Government and workers away from management as envisaged in Labour's Programme was inevitably unwelcome. British newspapers, largely owned by the business community campaigned in its interests as was to be expected. Whitehall was integrated into the business community through regular meetings, personal friendship and, for some, hope of future financial gain: the integration was of a degree unappreciated in the outside world. Senior officials were totally committed to the free market cluster of policies. Incapable of the detachment needed to distinguish the national interest they fought shamelessly and often shabbily for the business cause.

The Labour movement, equally unsurprisingly, supported the interventionist position. Labour stands for the maintenance of public expenditure to fund the public services — health, education, housing and social, and safeguards the jobs of those in the public sector. The re-industrialisation programme promised jobs and prosperity in the future. Planned trade would have maintained public expenditure and employment through the investment period.

Over a period, Labour Ministers systematically implemented the free market strategy.

The Key Decisions

During 1974 the Cabinet conducted a very limited renegotiation with the EEC, ignoring the vital issue of Britain's needs to fend off competition from European industry. Then, at the beginning of 1975, it decided to join the Tories and Liberals in recommending a 'Yes' vote in the Referendum — in direct opposition to the NEC — and, as it later transpired to the majority of the Parliamentary Labour Party. The Referendum result, three-to-two in favour of staying in the EEC, was then used to rule out any possibility of Britain adopting import controls or tough industrial intervention.

Meanwhile, the Party's industrial policy, which could have been used to reverse Britain's weak manufacturing position, was watered down. The NEB was hedged about with restrictions to prevent its use as a means of take-over. Planning Agreements were rendered a dead letter and trade union rights to information on company plans were tightly restricted. At the same time, cash was injected into faltering private companies on a massive scale by virtually exempting them from Corporation Tax and by writing escape clauses into the price controls inherited from the Conservatives. By the time Labour's Industry Act became law in the summer of 1975, it had been nullified as a means of compelling large companies to put their disastrous manufacturing performance to rights.

The basic dilemma as regards the trade deficit was not fully appreciated by the Government in 1974 when OPEC money poured into sterling and some Cabinet members thought Britain could 'borrow its way through'. But by the end of the year it was clear that a borrowing strategy could not continue. The Cabinet was presented with proposals for its first package of public expenditure cuts early in 1975, designed to cut the trade deficit and bolster confidence in sterling. At that point an alternative strategy, based on import controls and exchange controls to defend sterling without cutting spending in Britain, was first argued within the Government. But Ministers already pledged to the OECD not to intervene in trade and already for the most part committed to the EEC, rejected the alternative strategy and consented to the cuts, even though this would boost unemployment which by then had started to rise.

One final issue remained. So long as the Government relied on the goodwill of trade union members to seek a gradual abatement of inflation, it would be exposed to the risk that trade unions would eventually insist on alternative strategy, so far rejected, in order to protect jobs, public services and living standards when the effects of the existing strategy became clear. The social contract approach therefore threatened to undermine decisions already taken on the EEC, industrial intervention, public expenditure and import controls. Yet a statutory incomes policy for which Whitehall yearned seemed, after Heath, out of the question. The dilemma was resolved suddenly and dramatically in July 1975. TUC leaders were induced to acquiesce in the rough justice of a non-statutory wage policy under the secret threat of an imminent collapse of sterling and of a reserve, statutory policy.

When the TUC acquiesced in the £6 wages

policy, they handed over most of their bargaining power and became powerless to prevent the framework of policies which made high unemployment inevitable. From then on the Government had only one way to cope with Britain's industrial weakness causing low exports and rising imports. The cure to which the Cabinet subsequently resorted, time and time again, was cuts in public expenditure to deflate the economy. In effect, imports were rationed from 1975 onwards by the crude expedient of cutting living standards so that people had less money to spend on everything. The continuing de-industrialisation caused by this policy was such that when North Sea oil came on stream in 1976, its benefits were entirely offset by Britain's loss of manufactured trade. The oil-based boom, on the basis of which Labour might have hoped to win an election, never materialised and mass unemployment became endemic.

The Underlying Question

The deeper question of how the Labour Party came to be in the extraordinary position of being led by men and women who would not carry out its policies, and why the leadership of the Party could not intervene to correct matters is outside the scope of this article.

Part of the answer lies in the historical development of the Labour Party, part in the use of patronage by an existing leadership to perpetuate itself, part in the lack of any mechanism by which the Parliamentary leadership could be held accountable.

The secrecy surrounding Government work combined with the ruthless use by the Establishment of propaganda in support of free market policies to blank out coherent consideration of alternatives. Newspapers and television glamourised supporters of establishment policies and vilified those who supported the Labour interest.

V

Public Expenditure: The Retreat From Keynes

John Hughes

"Any widening of state activity is looked upon by 'business' with suspicion, but the creation of employment by government spending has a special aspect which makes the opposition particularly intense. Under a laissez-faire system the level of employment depends to a great extent on the so-called state of confidence. If this deteriorates, private investment declines, which results in a fall in output and employment . . . This gives the capitalists a powerful indirect control over government policy: everything which may shake the state of confidence must be carefully avoided because it would cause an economic crisis. But once the government learns the trick of increasing employment by its own purchases, this powerful controlling device loses its effectiveness. Hence budget deficits necessary to carry out government intervention must be regarded as perilous. The social function of the doctrine of 'sound finance' is to make the level of employment dependent on the 'state of confidence'."

M. Kalecki: *Political Aspects of Full Employment* (1943)

From 1976 the Labour government retreated further and further from anything resembling a full employment strategy. Some thirty five years ago Kalecki foresaw that persistent pressures from an alliance of business interests and "boom tired" rentier interests would be likely to produce a managed semi-slump economy. To re-read his analysis is to be presented with an evaluation and a criticism of our contemporary economy.

Whereas Conservative Governments have, hitherto, been prepared to take greater risks with business confidence, it has been the historic role of recent Labour Governments to deflate government spending persistently to offset a period of rising activity in the private sector of the economy. In this way the economy was presumably meant to avoid the economic tensions, and balance of payments difficulties, of 'peak' levels of trade cycle activity and relatively full employment. But to 'achieve' this is to 'achieve' also a heavy cost in terms of under-employed resources, and an ever more serious cost in terms of unemployment. In the period of deflation of public expenditure and reduction of budget deficits from 1967 to 1970, this meant that unemployment for the first time in the post-war years persisted at the (then) unusually high level of just over half a million. In the period of deflation of public expenditure and reduction of budget deficits since 1975 it has meant that unemployment has persisted at over one and a quarter million.

The White Paper on *The Government's Expenditure Plans: 1979-80 to 1982-83* offered no relief to the unemployed. Far from it; the unemployment figures for December 1978 (showing just over one and a quarter million, seasonally adjusted, unemployed in Great Britain) can fairly reliably be taken as the unemployment trough for this trade cycle. The White Paper offered no new perspective, and no let up in the retreat from

PUBLIC EXPENDITURE

Keynes and the attempt to manage a full employment economy.

Nevertheless, it is important that the "Expenditure Plans" White Paper should be closely analysed, to understand more fully what it tells us about the recent management of the economy, and what it indicates (however imprecisely) about the official stance on the future handling of public spending. It is necessary also to challenge some of the statements as well as some of the analysis that the White Paper offers.

Once again, the White Paper provides some further revision of earlier estimates of the extent of the fall in public expenditure — particularly between 1976 and 1978 — and of the very large scale of "shortfall" or under-spending in relation to planned programmes. The key elements are as follows:-

a. Compared with the previous fiscal year, public expenditure *fell* by about 2½% in 1976-77, and by as much as *7% in 1977-78.* This is a significantly greater fall than that estimated in earlier White Papers.

b. In 1976-77 planned expenditure was meant to be slightly higher than in the previous year. "Under-spending" turned out to be over £2 billion, about 3½% of the total. Much of this shortfall in spending was in categories (programmes for industry and employment, roads, transport, housing, etc.) directly affecting the level of demand in the economy. But the most staggering scale of under-spending turned out to be in 1977-78. Actual expenditure is now estimated to have been over £4 billion (about 7%) below the plans for that year. The categories of shortfall directly affecting the level of demand were only slightly greater than in the previous year. But the large shortfall of nationalised industry borrowing is directly connected with a further major fall in capital investment by public corporations, which was also demand deflationary. (The question of the rate of shortfall in 1978-79 is discussed subsequently.)

c. When we look at direct spending on goods and services in the economy, it becomes apparent that most of the weight of this decline in public spending fell on fixed investment. The figures are not given in the White Paper, but from the latest CSO estimates a continued and in total massive fall in such capital investment spending since 1974 becomes apparent.

General Government: Fixed Capital Formation
(In 1975 Constant Prices)

	£ million	Index 1975 = 100
1974	5,578	112
1975	4,974	100
1976	4,696	98
1977	3,854	77
1978*	(3,500)	(70)

*Estimate based on first three quarters, seasonally adjusted, annualised.

d. There was a very marked decline in the proportion of such direct public expenditures to the total Gross Domestic Product after 1975. Between 1974 and 1975 the proportion had risen slightly, as the real level of government expenditure rose slightly (in a Keynesian fiscal system it would have been expected to rise more) and as the level of activity in the rest of the economy fell back in the recession. But since 1975 the fall has been persistent and pronounced. This has arisen from virtually unchanged levels of public expenditure on "current goods and services", the fall in public capital spending that has been noted in the preceding paragraph, and the rise in levels of real output and expenditure in the rest of the economy.

The White Paper publishes a table on this, related to fiscal years.

General Government Expenditure on Goods and Services as a Ratio of Gross Domestic Product at Market Prices

From Expenditure White Paper		*From National Accounts*	
1974-1975	26%	1974	25.5
1975-1976	27%	1975	27.1
1976-1977	26%	1976	26.1
1977-1978	24%	1977	24.1
1978-1979 (est.)	23½%	1978	23.2
		(First 3 qrts.)	

Note: General government expenditure consists of spending on "current" goods and services and spending on "capital" formation. (This should not be confused with "total public expenditure", which includes transfer payments. According to the White Paper total public spending fell as a ratio of Gross Domestic Product from 46½% in 1975-76 to an estimated 42% in 1978-79).

Unfortunately the above estimate for 1978-79

appears to be too high (a point that will be pursued in more detail subsequently in this paper). Using the same categories and definitions it is possible to construct an equivalent table by calendar years and for the first three quarters of 1978, from national income annual and quarterly data.

e. It is instructive to look at the experience of this same range of years not in terms of the falling ratio of such spending but by contrasting the "real" (constant 1975 prices) changes in both public spending on goods and services and the performance in real terms of all the rest of the economy. What emerges very clearly from this is the heavily deflationary bias of public expenditure — most strikingly in 1977 — and the relatively vigorous real growth of the rest of the economy. It is consequently the handling of public expenditure since the recession that has resulted in the relatively low growth rates of the economy since the recession (thus in the year 1977 total gross domestic product was only 1.3% higher than the year before), and has meant that unemployment continued to mount.

Year to Year Changes at 1975 Constant Prices

	General Government Expenditure on goods & services	The rest of the Economy*
1974 to 1975	+2.1%	−3.2%
1975 to 1976	+0.7%	+4.7%
1976 to 1977	−3.4%	+3.0%
1977 to 1978 (1st 3 Qtrs.)	−0.2%	+5.1%

*This consists simply of gross domestic product at market prices *minus* general government expenditure on goods and services. The measure of GDP, as in the previous table, is based on the expenditure data in the national accounts.

Source: Calculated from CSO: *National Income and Expenditure, and Economic Trends,* January 1979.

f. It is important to recognise that the continuation of public sector financing deficits, and of a large (though reduced) public sector borrowing requirement, reflect the problems of an economy with serious deficiency of effective demand, operating well below full employment. This has the effect of increasing public expenditure, notably on the unemployed, but also on various forms of industrial aid (e.g., subsidisation of industrial investment), while curtailing revenue. Indeed, every deflationary effort by the government has to take this into account. Cuts in spending have to be greater than the desired reduction in (say) the public sector borrowing requirements, since the extra deflation they push into the economy will raise unemployment and therefore curtail tax revenue and raise the expenditure on benefits.

Various estimates have been made of the scale of this effect on the public sector's financial outturn from a depressed economy. For instance the National Institute of Economic and Social Research (*Economic Review,* May 1977, p.17) calculated that in 1976 the gap between the level of activity in the economy and the level of gross domestic product that would have been enjoyed in a 'high employment' situation was nearly 8%. The actual public sector financial deficit was (at rather over £8 billion) around 8% of the total gross domestic product. The same structure of taxation and spending would in a 'high employment' situation have reduced the financial deficit by over £5 billion to some £3 billion or just under 3% of the gross domestic product. For 1977 the Institute calculated an even bigger swing to public sector surplus were the economy to operate at a 'high employment' level. Thus, in some ways, the retreat from a high employment economy multiplies the problems of public sector finance.

Public Spending: What Happened in 1978-79?

It must be emphasised that on information available so far it does *not* appear as if the fiscal year 1978-79 marked any measurable return to the restoration of the function of public expenditure as a support to the growth of the economy, the real improvement of the social wage, or the raising of the level of employment. This is despite the fact that at an earlier stage the *plans* for 1978-79 appeared to offer a serious prospect of renewed growth of public spending in real terms.

At this stage the following features of public spending in 1978-79 appear to be important:-

a. The White Paper on the government's expenditure plans still appeared to be assuming a sizeable increase in public spending at constant prices. The *planning* totals for 1978-79 compared with those for 1977-78, however, only show a

2% increase, i.e., one well below the growth rate of the rest of the economy. But the government projections of actual "outturn" were based on an arbitrary assumption that the "shortfall" (of actual expenditure as compared with planned spending) was going to be reduced in 1978-79 to £2 billion. In the previous fiscal year, 1977-78 the shortfall is now estimated — as has been noted already — at over £4 billion. It should be said, in this context, that official projections have persistently under-estimated the amount of shortfall in public spending.

b. Estimates of the growth in public spending need to be examined with care since special factors affected the 1977-78 figures. For instance, the sale of BP shares in 1977-78 reduces the total for that year, but does not represent by itself any change in effective demand for currently produced goods and services. There were major falls in nationalised industry borrowing in 1977-78 as well. The official calculation is that leaving aside such special factors (which do not affect the normal pattern of expenditure either directly on goods and services, or on transfer payments) the increase in public spending from 1977-78 to 1978-79 is "at present" expected to be no more than 2½% to 3%.

c. In fact, the available evidence shows no such increase in public expenditure in real terms coming through. For the increase assumed in the White Paper to appear would require a marked acceleration in the second half of the fiscal year

— and there is no evidence of this. Let us take first of all the quarterly data (from the CSO) for general government spending in the first half of the 1978-79 fiscal year (the second and third quarters of 1978) compared with the same period of the previous year.

General Government Expenditure: Middle Quarters of 1977 and 1978

(1975 Constant Prices. Seasonally adjusted)

			£ million
Period	Current Goods & services	Fixed Capital Formation	Combined Total
1977 II	5,841	944	6,785
1977 III	5,827	928	6,755
1978 II	5,907	850	6,757
1978 III	5,909	881	6,790
Percentage change 1977 (II & III) to 1978 (II & III)	+1.3%	−7.5%	+0.05%

Note: No estimate is available for change in stocks and work in progress, but this is always a very small item for the general government sector.

Give or take the uncertainties of subsequent revision, these statistics indicate no overall growth at all in the components of public spending that represent direct demand for goods and services. A slow rise in spending on 'current' goods and services has been offset by a decline in capital spending. Nor is this decline in 'general government' capital spending compensated for by any rise in public corporations' fixed capital spending, for this actually declined (in 1975 prices) by nearly 10% over the same period. What is more, one important forward indicator of public sector capital spending, that for public sector housing starts, shows a continuing fall later in 1978. The October-November 1978 levels were *over 30% below* those of the same months in 1977.

Consequently, it must be concluded that any 'real' increase in public expenditure in 1978-79 came about almost entirely from increases in the 'real' value of current grants (transfer payments) and influences the economy through increased real disposable income in the hands of recipients of pensions, benefits, and the like.

This Year, Next Year, Sometime . . .

There is little in the survey so far made of public expenditure planning and actual performances since the recession of 1975 to inspire confidence in the White Paper's projections for the period ahead. On the contrary, in the White Paper itself and in subsequent announcements there was ample evidence that the role of public expenditure in helping to sustain a high employment economy had been largely abandoned. It is both a problem of the reasoning and objectives behind the government's spending 'plans' and a problem of the loss of control over (or wilful 'shortfall' against) those plans. The savage deflation of housing starts in the public sector (mainly local authority) that has just been noted provides an example; the White Paper barely notices what is happening, and avoids any expression of disapproval. Cash limits may control any *over*-fulfilment of plans but under-fulfilment

— even in exaggerated form — is apparently tolerated.

In essence, the future expenditure plans put forward by the government were "less than accommodating" to the needed growth of the national economy. It is true that "less than accommodating" was the revealing phrase used by the government itself to identify its monetary policies in the event of double figure increases in earnings. But it will stand well enough as identifying the general approach to its public spending policies overall. It is necessary to argue why this did indeed appear to be the government's attitude:-

i. The government, on somewhat uncertain evidence, put the "productive potential" of the economy at no more than around or slightly above three per cent per annum. What is meant by the phrase "productive potential" is the rate of growth of gross domestic product consistent with a *constant* level of unemployment. It is far from clear that the "productive potential" is as low as that. Thus, in the decade 1964-74 the underlying rate of increase of labour productivity (output per head) was two and three quarters per cent per annum. In the years of economic crisis and under-employment from 1974 to 1977 this rate fell — not surprisingly — to around one and three quarters per cent per annum. Recession, under-employment of capital equipment, arbitrary cuts in public spending, are likely to have that kind of adverse effect on labour productivity. But the government built its estimate for the years from 1977 to 1982 on a rise in output per head (for the economy excluding North Sea Oil) on a depressed forecast range of no more than one and a half per cent to two and a quarter per cent.

ii. The uncertainties of such projections are compounded by the delay on the part of the government in producing even its 1977 employment census. What the earlier census had revealed was a rapid increase in part-time employment (outside the production industries); in other words part of the alleged slow down in the rate of increase of labour productivity may be due to a disproportionate increase in part-time, rather than full time employment. To put it another way, it is hardly a reasonable way of measuring the "productive potential" of the system not to notice that more of the employment consists of part-timers rather than full-timers.

iii. The government's view of the rate of growth required to match the growth in "productive potential" was built up around three components which may be under-estimated:

  a. Assumed growth in the labour force of half per cent per annum. This would almost certainly be higher (given the demographic pattern and the long period tendency for the proportion of women in the working age groups who join the labour force to rise) if more jobs were on offer.

    b. Productivity; which might be expected to be at the upper end of the assumed range of one and a half per cent to two and a quarter per cent or even higher.

    c. The contribution of North Sea Oil and gas to the growth in GDP, estimated at three quarter per cent per annum.

Thus it is reasonable to assume that productive potential should be assumed to rise at around three and a half per cent per annum.

iv. But "productive potential" does not indicate what growth rate of the economy should be *aimed at*. To aim at — or achieve — no more than a growth in line with "productive potential" would mean leaving unemployment at its current appallingly high level (around one and a third million or more). At the very least one might assume that to make major inroads into the total unemployment in the system it would be necessary to aim at a rate of growth of the total domestic product higher than "productive potential", that is four per cent per annum or higher.

v. So far from this being the case, only the most favourable of the government's "illustrative" estimates for the "medium term" assumed as such as a three per cent per annum growth in gross domestic product.

vi. However, even this is assuming a relatively high rate of increase of private sector and nationalised industry expenditure over the "medium term". For the public expenditure plans only provided for a total increase of about two per cent a year in real terms over the next four years. An even lower rate of increase was assumed for that part of the government and local authority spending that falls directly on goods and services. Spending on "current" goods and services was only planned to rise by one and three quarter per cent a year; the provision for capital expenditure provided for no increase at all. Capital expenditure was planned, we were told in the White Paper, to remain "broadly constant" over the planning period. To put that another way, capital expenditure in the early 1980s in real terms was being "planned" at no more than around two-thirds of the 1974 and 1975 levels of annual expenditure. Overall, the part of general government spending that relates to direct purchase of goods and services was only planned to expand at one and a half per cent per annum. This means that the government was assuming that the total of private sector expenditure would rise at the rate of three and a half per cent a year. Given the normally cyclical pattern of private sector activity and the fact that (as was noted earlier) quite high rates of expansion of private sector expenditure have been recorded since the recession of 1975 this assumption of a sustained three and a half per cent real growth seems high. But notice, that to attain the four per cent a year growth of the economy that might offer some prospect of steady decline in unemployment, the private sector of the economy would need to expand by nearly five per cent per annum (still assuming only a one and a half per cent increase per annum for public spending directly on goods and services). It is palpably clear that the public spending plans offered no support at all to growth rates that might hold out hope for the unemployed.

vii. The *Plans* therefore left it to the private sector to provide most of the increase in effective demand that can generate economic growth. But, it may well be that the outlook was worse than these planning figures suggest. Was there any serious intention to carry out the plan?

The *appearance* in the White Paper of "planning" for even a two per cent growth in overall public spending was achieved by two dubious means:

— The further assumption is made that there will be an annual "shortfall" of £2 billion a year. This seems to be the perpetual tribute we must pay to the "cash limit" system. In practice, even this may be an under-estimate of "shortfall" of actual spending below the planned levels. Thus the programme figures are set down *before* allowance for this "shortfall". And the "shortfall" may still be under-estimated.

— Substantially larger amounts each year are not allocated to programmes at all but added to the "contingency reserve", which is increased in the plans by £500 to £600 million each year to reach as much as £2,500 millions by 1982-83.

Suppose we try to work back to what the government had provided for in programmed spending to 1982-83, subtracting from the *apparent* totals the assumed under-spend and the "contingency reserve". Then, at 1978 survey prices, all that was provided for was an increase in "programmed" spending from around £62 billion in 1978-79 to around £65 billion by 1982-83 (estimated from Tables 1, 2, and 14 of the White Paper). This represented no more than a provision for an *annual increase in programmed expenditure of 1.2%.*

viii. However, this is still subject to the caveat that has already been emphasised: we appear under the cash limits system to be operating with a persistent tendency to underspend in relation to planned programmes. It is by no means clear that a £2 billion a year (at 1978 survey prices) allowance for this is adequate.

ix. In addition we are, in 1979, facing an interpretation of the role of public expenditure which in the government's classic phrase is "less than accommodating" to the growth of the national economy. In other words, not only is monetary growth so organised as to reduce the rate of economic growth generally, but cash limits are (as we now discover) to be set in a deliberately restrictive way. Despite the obscurities of the government's statement on cash limits, it is apparent that it intended to force a trade-off between pay increases in the public sector and the level of public sector (and service) real expenditure and employment.

Without doubt, therefore, the total implications of the White Paper and of subsequent government statements were persistently deflationary. By any standards, the government was setting an expected rate of growth that makes no inroads into the army of the unemployed. Even in that stance it was planning public spending on the assumption that the private sector's effective demand would expand significantly faster than the public's. And, finally nothing in the history of cash limits or recent statements as to their future role gave any confidence that there would not be both a downward pressure on the "real" level of public spending from the limits themselves and an excessive "shortfall" of actual expenditure below the limits set.

All this has to be set against an economy with deteriorating prospects for growth, partly as a result of governmental policies and partly for other reasons. The events in Iran are ensuring that 1979 at least will be more inflationary but also more demand deflationary than would earlier have been expected (for the world economy, not just for Britain). The successive increase in interest rates of recent months will add to both these effects (i.e., a higher rate of price inflation; demand deflated) so far as Britain is concerned. Loss of output and to some extent effective demand as a result of widespread industrial disputes and settlement delays operate similarly. On top of all this the Government was seeking to lower the Public Sector Borrowing Requirement by the same device it used in 1976 and 1977, by pushing up nationalised industry prices (as a substitute for the raising of indirect taxes); once again, the effect is price inflationary and demand deflationary.

Britain was therefore from all these directions (and not simply, as the media will insist, from pay push) risking a return to double figure inflation rates. At the same time the expected growth rate of the economy needs to be revised downward. It is unlikely to match "productive potential" which is another way of saying that unemployment can be expected to rise through the year (probably somewhat erratically). This is the context within which the late Government's policy has to be judged.

But was it unavoidable?

However, it might be argued that tragic as this survey of public expenditure has been, it was the necessary price for "sound" management of the economy. In earlier years we heard much of the "crowding out" of private sector use of resources by increased public sector claims on them. We heard too of the alleged dangers of high levels of public sector financing deficits for management of the monetary system.

At almost the same time as an earlier White Paper on *The Government's Expenditure Plans* the OECD published its December 1977 edition of *Economic Outlook*. This had a very interesting, if guardedly written, "special section" on "Public Sector Indebtedness and Government Financing". What it showed is that the UK was not alone in the increase in its financing deficit (as measured by the public sector borrowing requirement) between the boom of 1973 and the recession of 1975; the increase in the deficit was about the same — measured as a proportion of Gross Domestic Product — in the USA, in Japan and in Germany (an increase of around 5% of GDP). Since 1975 both Britain and Germany emerge as countries that hastened to curtail their public sector deficits (and in both slow growth and rising unemployment are to be observed), whereas the United States and Japan showed a more modest reversal of their public sector financial deficits. But in none of the countries studied was there a "crowding out" problem or any major difficulty in financing the deficit:

> "The financing of increased public sector indebtedness has been made relatively easy in recent years by the concomitant cyclical weakness in private sector demands for credit. Since the total supply of credit market funds available for meeting private and public sector demands has remained stable or even increased, there was little internal pressure on interest rates." (OECD, *Economic Outlook*, December 1977, p.43.)

Nor did any serious problems emerge in the handling of the public debt: "the monetisation of government debt was well contained in all countries considered, and tendencies towards shortening maturity structures of outstanding government debt were quickly reversed". And the OECD went on to give a small but distinct cheer for Keynesian fiscal policy (having shown that the orthodox monetarist fears of deficit financing had not been borne out):-

> "Present levels of public indebtness and government financing needs as such do not appear, on purely economic grounds, to stand in the way of employment-supporting fiscal policies in the largest OECD economies." (*op.cit.*, page 46.)

It is a sad comment on the Government's White Paper on its expenditure plans that it did not even move as far as the OECD back to a cautious acceptance of Keynesian fiscal logic.

As Keynes said, policies of cutting expenditure and balancing budgets in a period of recession meant that resources were "released . . . to stand at street corners and draw the dole". The legacy of the lurch back to pre-Keynesian Treasury orthodoxies since 1975 is there not only in reduced public services, unkempt and obsolete public buildings, and potholes in the roads, but in an additional half a million or so unemployed workers.

VI

Whatever Happened to Industrial Democracy?

Ken Coates

The years of the Heath administration provoked a great radicalisation of the trade unions. First, the Industrial Relations Act of 1971 brought them on to the streets, to begin with in vast official demonstrations, and later in a spontaneous outburst of collective rage, when the first victims of the Act made their way into prison. Second, the policy of allowing industrial "lame ducks" to die off provoked the work-in of Upper Clyde Shipbuilders in 1971, and this triggered an unprecedented movement of work-ins, sit-ins and general strike actions in defence of jobs, all of which had the direct effect of making an issue of the rights of workers to be involved in strategic decision-making, and some of which directly posed the question of workers' control. Third, successive conflicts over pay policies provoked more and more fraught conflicts, involving millions of people, and culminating in an enforced three-day week, followed by a miners' strike and a General Election in which the Government finally fell.

Seldom has the British Establishment lost its nerve so completely as during those days. When

Mr Wilson re-formed a minority Labour administration, there was little it could not have done to secure the democratic reform of industry had it only had the will. The fact that the Conservatives had deliberately set out to curb the powers of the trade union interest, and overridden all opposition, was a clear and open invitation to Labour to respond by rolling back those irresponsible powers of capital against which various Labour leaders had fulminated at a long succession of mayday celebrations and miners' gala festivals. This, however, was not Mr Wilson's intention: the Establishment having come adrift from its moorings, his one overriding instinct was to spatchcock it back into place again. The lid had been blown off the British industrial/political system, and the third-time Labour premier saw himself as exactly the man to rivet it back on again.

With a little help from his friends, this is precisely what he did.

*   *   *

On the morning of Tuesday, October 2nd 1973, Ken Fleet, who was delegated by his (Beeston) Labour Party, but who is better-known as the secretary of the Institute for Workers' Control, went to the rostrum at the Party's Annual Conference in Blackpool, to move a composite resolution on Industrial Democracy. After a debate in which a number of leading spokesmen participated, including Eric Heffer, Roy Jenkins, Michael Meacher and others, his motion was approved so overwhelmingly that no one called for a card vote.

The motion began with what at the time was almost a ritual salute to Tony Benn's celebrated watchword, committing the Party to "a fundamental and irreversible shift in the balance of wealth and power, in favour of the working people and their families". It went on to spell out a quite specific range of measures:

> "Conference welcomes the determination to extend public ownership and control, especially in the key growth sectors of the economy, but is convinced that for this policy to be carried through successfully, to win widespread support and to become the basis for fundamental changes in the social structure, strong and genuine elements of industrial democracy and workers' control will have to be introduced in all nationalised industries. It is essential that structures be imposed which will allow for the full exercise of the talents and democratic rights of the workers in those companies, that these include the direct election of trades unionists at all levels under arrangements agreed with and supervised by the trades unions concerned; the Board of each nationalised industry must be composed of at least 50 per cent trades unionists elected in this way, and workers must have the right of veto over all executive appointments including that of the chairman. Workers' representatives must have equal rights and powers with other members of these boards and complete access to all information concerning their industries and enterprises and be required to report back fully to their constituents and be subject to recall by these constituents."

The intervention of Roy Jenkins in this discussion was a remarkably nervous and cautious one. He spoke with a considerable passion, to insist that

> "We need to promise no more than we are convinced we can do."

INDUSTRIAL DEMOCRACY

At the same time, Roy Jenkins gave the studied impression that he had no objection to the extension of democracy into public sector industries:

> "It is no good taking over a vast number of industries without a clear plan as to how and by whom they are to be run. It is no good pretending a transfer of ownership in itself solves our problems."

In reply to this and other interventions, Tony Benn, speaking for the Executive, went out of his way to widen the argument: accepting that "nationalisation plus Lord Robens does not add up to socialism", he called for a bold response: "industrial democracy begins now", he said . . . "if we are only concerned to win the votes we shall never mobilise the strength we need to implement the policy . . . if we win the argument we shall win the election". "We are offering much more than legislation", he went on: "we are offering a perspective and a vision which will transform the political atmosphere of cynicism which has developed in recent years. Without a vision people will turn to their immediate and narrow self-interests. With some sense that they are part of a change in our society we shall be able to draw much more from them . . ." If this was a response to Mr Jenkins previous plea not to "add to the dangerous public disillusionment with parties, with politics and with politicians", Tony Benn's next remark was directed at future adversaries rather than past ones:

> "One delegate said that we shall inherit a crisis when we come to power. We are saying . . . that the crisis that we

inherit when we come to power will be the occasion for fundamental change and not the excuse for postponing it."

It was with these words in their minds that Labour activists went into the two election campaigns of 1974. Although they have since been falsified by events, there is a very real sense in which their implied reproach is a theme for every count in the indictment of this little book.

The October 1974 Election Manifesto contained an explicit pledge to honour the decisions previously reached in this and other Labour Party Conferences. "We will", it said, "introduce new legislation to help forward our plans for a radical extension of industrial democracy in both the private and public sectors. This will involve major changes in company law and in the statutes which govern the nationalised industries and the public services". Already in February 1974, the previous Manifesto had pledged "We intend to socialise the nationalised industries. In consultation with the unions, we shall take steps to make the management of existing nationalised industries more responsible to the workers in the industry and more responsive to their consumers' needs".

For a brief while it appeared as though Tony Benn's formula for meeting "the crisis that we shall inherit" was capable of application. With the repeal of the Industrial Relations Act of 1971, the tabling of the Employment Protection Act, and a variety of other measures, the defensive needs of the Trades Union Congress were swiftly met, at any rate in substantial measure. Hopes of democratic innovation were held out by the funding (albeit inadequately) of three worker cooperatives in collapsing private sector enterprises: at Meriden, Triumph Motorcycles; at Kirkby, KME, manufacturing radiators and a range of other products; and the *Scottish Daily News* in Glasgow. Bitter fights between ministers (and above all, the Secretary of State for Industry, Tony Benn himself) and senior civil servants became daily events during these days. And the Industry Act was battled through, clause by clause, as is described in Chapter III by Tom Forester.

Then, with the defeat of the Labour Party, at the hands of a coalition embracing most of its own Government and virtually the entire political and media Establishments, in the Referendum on membership of the European Economic Community, came the counter-revolution. Tony Benn was instantly dismissed from his department, and given Energy instead. Various others were removed. Eric Heffer had already been pushed out before the Referendum had taken place. The Industry Act was next instantly filleted by Prime Ministerial command. New co-operatives were nipped in the bud by allowing the work-ins at Imperial Typewriters in Hull and Norton Villiers Triumph to sink unaided, and by installing Eric Varley at the Department of Industry. (Mr Varley, who as a mineworker had been an effective partisan of workers' control, has shown a remarkable political consistency. When he became a Member of Parliament, he favoured Parliamentary control, and once he was a Minister, he was immediately converted to ministerial control. The unifying principle, as may be readily seen, is the appealingly simple one of Varley's control. Unhappily, this is a Platonic ideal. Whilst showing great virtuosity in the pursuit of office Mr Varley seems to have no particular ideas about how to employ it once obtained.)

Having thus met the demand of fundamental change head-on, Harold Wilson then set about postponing it indefinitely. In August 1975 Peter Shore announced the intention to appoint a committee of enquiry on whether or not the Election Manifestos were to be carried out:

> "Accepting the need for a radical extension of industrial democracy in the control of companies by means of representation on boards of directors, and accepting the essential role of trade union organisations in this process, to consider how such an extension can best be achieved, taking into account in particular the proposals of the Trades Union Congress report on industrial democracy as well as experience in Britain, the EEC and other countries. Having regard to the interest of the national economy, employees, investors and consumers, to analyse the implications of such representation for the efficient management of companies and for company law."

It took until December to find an appropriate mix of experts to staff this committee: and then after that it took until January 1977 for the subsequent *Report* to be agreed and published. The policy of the TUC, following upon the circulation, during Mr Heath's administration, of the EEC's fifth directive, (which proposed a modified form of co-determination on the lines of German company law, as a possible European standard) had been to press for a 50% share of company direction. Lord Bullock's Committee, which included three representatives of the TUC (Jack Jones, Clive Jenkins and David Lea) also involved three company chairmen (Mr Norman Biggs of Williams and Glyn's bank; Sir Jack Callard of ICI; Mr Barrie Heath of Guest, Keen and Nettlefolds Ltd.) and a sprinkling of lawyers and academics, one of whom (John Methven) was to leave the newly appointed Committee in order to become director of the Confederation of British Industry. It was perfectly clear that this mix had been designed in order to encourage a watering down of the TUC's inconvenient ideas. This was duly accomplished, although to a lesser extent that was probably intended. The Committee recommended in favour of parity control of the larger companies only, but with an intervening group of mutually acceptable "independents" holding the balance. This was the "$2x + y$" formula, which, accompanied by a great deal of small print, helped to secure a certain loss of interest among the shop stewards whose active pressure alone could ensure the success of the scheme. The most effective and carefully worked out part of the Report concerned the problem of co-ordinating workpeople's trade union representation within firms, but, sage though this was (reflecting the draftsmanship of Jack Jones himself and Bill Wedderburn?) it was generally overlooked in the dispute which then broke out between the major unions. The Engineers (AUEW), normally fiercely divided between left and right factions, showed a united front against the proposals. They were followed by the electricians (EETPU), and, at a discreet and less intransigent distance, by the General and Municipal Workers. It was no small feat of management on the part of Jack Jones that he held the TUC consensus through all such divisions. The 1977 Congress approved a resolution in these terms:

"This Congress welcomes the analysis of the Bullock Committee Report highlighting the need for industrial democracy and reaffirms its belief in legislative action in this field. This does not assume that the only way forward is to legislate for worker representation on the policy-making boards of companies. This Congress is convinced that collective bargaining can be extended to greatly increase trade union influence over main policies. The extension of worker representation on policy boards or committees should not be used as a means of frustrating the processes of existing collective bargaining machinery. Congress calls upon the Government to legislate for full disclosure of information necessary to enable trade union representatives to properly represent their members.

In order to maintain maximum unity within the trade union Movement on this issue, Congress calls upon the General Council to press the Labour Government to provide for statutory backing to all unions wishing to establish joint control of strategic planning decisions via trade union machinery. This legislation would include the option of parity representation on the board, but would also link up with more flexible forms of joint regulation more clearly based on collective bargaining. Congress further believes that the objective of making the public sector of industry serve social purposes will be strengthened by effective worker participation on management boards and urges immediate steps to implement the proposals of the Nationalised Industries Committee for parity trade union representation on the boards of nationalised industries where it is the wish of the members."

By now it was September.

Mr Edmund Dell, now Secretary for Trade, had promised legislation "during the 1977 session". It was clear that time was running short.

At the beginning of the following month, the Labour Party Conference approved a somewhat stronger resolution, from the Iron and Steel Trades Confederation, about the lack of progress in the Nationalized industries. This viewed

> "With concern the apparent lack of progress towards democracy in industry."

It went on to urge

> "the Government as an act of faith in Socialist principle to speedily implement the movement towards industrial democracy in the nationalised industries. Nevertheless Conference believes that participation must extend from the shop floor to the main board, be permitted to be flexible, allowing for the history of industrial relations in the industry concerned, and firmly based on the trade union machinery as an adjunct to traditional collective bargaining."

Something had been done about this in the Post Office, where a participatory top-level structure had been agreed, and active consultations did go ahead with the mineworkers. But in general, very little actually happened. This did not stop the circulation of minutes, however.

It was not until May 1978 that the discussions within the small circle of secretaries of state (Education, Employment, Trade: under the chairmanship of Shirley Williams, wearing her hat as Paymaster General) had reached the point where a white paper might be offered up. This wondered whether various things might be done: a code of practice might be drawn up by an Industrial Democracy Commission "if one is set up". Failing this, ACAS "might be invited to draw it up with a view to its being submitted to Parliament for approval". The one solid bone offered to the unions was that the Joint Representation Committees recommended by Bullock might be established, not to implement any prescribed reform, but in order to discuss company strategy. From a fundamental and irreversible shift in the balance of wealth and power, the circle had moved to show

> "the object of participation is understanding and co-operation . . . recourse to statutory fall-back arrangements will be the exception."

Board representation, but not on terms of parity, was to become a statutory right after an interim of "three to four years from the date of establishment of the Joint Representation Committee".

Even this limited object remained an aspiration. No legislative proposals were ever made, either in May 1978 or therafter.

Not surprisingly, the General Council did not mark this tepid document very high. They "considered that the Government were proposing a very protracted timetable for the attainment of . . . modest objectives".

The Prime Minister greeted the white paper with a hope that legislation might be tabled in the 1978-9 session. This would have brought the matter round to the mid-eighties before any notion of compulsion came into play. In November

1978 the Queen's Speech to a Parliament which was doomed to dissolution promised to legislate

> "to ensure that employees and unions were able to participate in discussions of corporate strategy, and to provide in due course for employee representation on company boards."

By April 1979 this had still not materialised.

At the beginning of this long process, the TUC had been calling for parity involvement in company boards, by which it meant 50% representation for workplace union representatives. By the time Bullock reported, the $2x + y$ formula had diluted the notion of parity, and the main union advance proposed was the establishment of effective JRCs, which could solve the problem of representation at combine level. In the white paper, the German system originally rejected by the TUC had now re-emerged, but with major adjustments towards the employers' interests. Parity had already become a "phased" target: it was difficult to see why any self-respecting shop steward should wish to embroil himself in such a stew of compromise and equivocation. Rank-and-file enthusiasm, diminished by each successive devaluation of the original project, was already moving towards zero quite some time before the Queen pronounced a promise of legislation that was never to come.

The strategy of company law reform, properly considered, may still have something to commend it to socialists: but it is doubtful whether the Bullock Report will ever be debated again. A much more apposite reform was proposed during 1971, at the time of the UCS work-in, by Tony Benn. It would simply have required, as an annual ritual upon which continued registration as a limited company would depend, the depositing of a certificate of acceptability signed by the relevant workpeople's representatives. This would enable the unions to negotiate whatever degree and style of participatory involvement seemed appropriate to them.

VII

How the Poor Fared

Frank Field, MP

A review of Labour's poverty record during the 1974-79 Parliaments needs to cover, amongs other things:

— How effective Labour policies were in combating poverty and so reducing the numbers of people who live on low incomes.

— How effective the same policies were in reducing the numbers of poor dependent on meanstested benefits.

— How effective were Labour's policies in narrowing the differences in living standards between the poor and the rest of the community.

— How effective were the policies in bringing about a fairer horizontal distribution of income (the vertical distribution of income is examined in Chapter II).

This essay will briefly review the evidence on each of these aspects of Labour's social policy before drawing together the lessons of the Party's social programme from 1974 to 1979.

COMBATING POVERTY

What is the poverty line?

There has been a major debate in this country on how we should define poverty in the post-war world. Criticisms have been made of the absolute definition of poverty which dominated Seebohm Rowntree's first study in York at the turn of the century. But before the first world war Rowntree was reshaping his definition of poverty into a more relative concept (the most forceful case for a relative definition is in P. Townsend (ed), *The Concept of Poverty*, Heinemann, 1970). It is this relative approach which dominates discussion today, and each year Parliament revises the minimum level of income for claimants dependent on supplementary benefit so as roughly to take account of rising living standards.

Many regard the supplementary benefit scale rates as an official definition of poverty. They certainly provide us with a generally accepted yardstick for discussion on the numbers in poverty, although there is a growing body of evidence on just how restricted living standards are for people existing on this level of income (see section 3 of Frank Field, *Poverty and Inequality: The Facts*, CPAG, 1979).

The official poverty line is determined by the supplementary benefit scale rates. An unemployed man with two children (one under five and one under ten) who happens to be paying an average rent of £6.50 is entitled to a supplementary benefit allowance — or poverty line income — of £41.45 (the 1978/9 rates). In individual day-to-day terms it means that a married couple must cover "all normal needs that can be foreseen, including food, fuel, light, the normal repair and replacement of clothing, household sundries (but not major items of bedding and furniture) and provision for amenities such as newspapers, entertainments and television licences" (*Supplementary Benefit Handbook*, HMSO, 1977, page 26), from an allowance of around £3.60 a day (after the rent has been paid), and are expected to keep their youngest child on 63p a day.

Numbers of poor

Taking these scale rates as the measurement of poverty, what is the record of the last Labour Government in combating the number of poor?

The most important source of data on the numbers of people on low incomes is the special analysis made of the Family Expenditure Survey (FES). This series began regular publication in 1972. But as the self-employed were not included in the analysis until 1974, the series is only comparable from that date. The latest information is for 1976 and from this data we can look at the number of people living on incomes below the Supplementary Benefit (SB) poverty line, on SB and on incomes up to 40 per cent about the SB scale rates.

The numbers of people living at an income below the official poverty line rose from 1,410,000 in 1974 to 2,280,000 in 1976 and, as we can see from the table below, the majority of these people in 1976 (1,410,000) were below pensionable age.

The numbers of persons who were normally in full-time work and earning less than they could get on SB rose from 130,000 to 290,000 in the period under study. If we include their dependants then the totals rise from 360,000 to 890,000 respectively. The years since 1974 have also seen an increase in the numbers of unemployed whose income is not brought up to the official supplementary benefit poverty line. In 1974 the survey recorded 40,000 in this position and by 1976 the numbers had risen to 100,000. By adding in their dependants we find that in the same period of time the totals rose from 90,000 to 170,000.

Not all the families in full-time work earning less than a poverty line income have children, but the majority of them do so. Overwhelmingly this group is composed of two-parent families — the sampling cells for one-parent families were so small that the estimates in the table are subject to wide margins of error. However, we do see a rise from 60,000 to 170,000 two-parent families who are normally in full-time work and earning less than the official poverty line. In 1976 these families were responsible for 390,000 children.

One note of caution: in one important respect these FES data underestimate the numbers of the very poorest for they exclude the near million souls living in institutions. Although these people are living on extremely low levels of income it is not possible to make comparison with their standard

Table 1: Numbers living below Supplementary Benefit level (excluding SB recipients)

	1974 Families	1974 Persons	1975 Families	1975 Persons	1976 Families	1976 Persons
	(thousands)					
Over pension age						
Married couples	90	200	140	280	160	320
Single persons	350	350	450	470	550	550
Total	450	550	590	740	700	870
Under pension age						
Married with children	90	390	170	700	190	820
Single with children	(20)	(70)	50	150	(40)	100
Married without children	(30)	(70)	80	170	70	130
Single without children	330	330	270	270	360	360
Total	470	850	560	1,280	650	1,410
Total	920	1,410	1,150	2,030	1,350	2,820

Source: House of Commons Hansard, Vol.919, Cols 1000-2, and 3 August 1978, Vol.955, Cols 271-6·; and DHSS (SR3) analysis of FES, 1975.

of living in an institution compared with those living on incomes up to the supplementary benefit poverty line. Nevertheless their numbers should be borne in mind when considering the size of the army of those who live around the minimum level of income approved by Parliament.

Table 2, which analyses the numbers found to be claiming supplementary benefits from the FES returns, gives a total which is less than that recorded in the annual reports of the Supplementary Benefits Commission. The FES data present average annual incomes. They tell us nothing about those who might have been very poor at a particular point during the year but whose annual income for the whole year brings them above the poverty line. The same is true for the numbers of claimants of supplementary benefit which are taken from the annual statistical enquiry of supplementary benefit claimants carried out on one day in December each year. But in order to present the number of claimants on a similar basis to the FES data the figures for supplementary benefit claimants are reworked to present an average annual number of claimants. The number for 1976 was 4,090,000. But the figure for the number of claimants on the actual day of the enquiry was some 600,000 higher at 4,725,000.

The FES data also classify those with incomes of up to 40 per cent more than the SB level. Three-fifths of the 8½ million people living on the margins of poverty were under pensionable age and over half were in households where the head was normally in full-time work. Further details of these groups and the record since 1974 are given in Table 3.

The growing vulnerability of children again emerges when the data are re-analysed according to age and marital status. Of the total of 8½ million living up to 40 per cent above the supplementary benefit level in 1976, 4,400,000 were married or single people and their children. The numbers of married people under pensionable age without children totalled 490,000 in 1976 and single people without children on incomes up to 40 per cent above the SB poverty line in that year totalled 390,000.

Rise in numbers of poor under Labour

It is now possible to look at the Labour Government's record in combating poverty. The data only allows us to consider the record up to 1976, but with unemployment continuing to rise, the numbers of single parent families increasing and the falling relative value of benefits in the years since then, it is doubtful if the record will appear in better light when the data for the remaining years become available.

The most depressing and shameful conclusion which emerges from this survey is the steady increase in the numbers of poor during this period of Labour Government and this is an increase which cannot totally be explained away by the increase in the relative value of the supplementary benefit poverty line as measured against net earnings. The main points to note are that for the years 1974 to 1976

Table 2: Families and persons receiving supplementary benefit, 1974-1976

	1974		1975		1976	
	Families	Persons	Families	Persons	Families	Persons
			(thousands)			
Over pension age						
Married couples	320	650	280	560	290	580
Single people	1,480	1,480	1,400	1,410	1,370	1,370
Total	1,810	2,130	1,680	1,960	1,660	1,950
Under pension age						
Married with children	80	390	120	550	140	640
Single with children	260	760	260	760	320	920
Married without children	80	150	70	130	80	160
Single without children	300	300	360	360	410	410
Total	720	1,600	810	1,810	950	2,140
Total	2,530	3,730	2,490	3,770	2,610	4,090

Source: House of Commons Hansard, 27 November 1976 and 1 August 1978.

Table 3: Number of families and persons with income within 140 per cent of the supplementary benefit level, 1974-1976

	1974 Families	1974 Persons	1975 Families	1975 Persons	1976 Families	1976 Persons
			(thousands)			
Under pensionable age						
Family head or single parent:						
a. normally in full-time work	620	2,320	860	3,290	1,230	4,450
b. sick or disabled for three months	90	290	120	300	130	290
c. unemployed for more than three months	90	180	80	190	120	290
d. others	440	610	200	340	190	290
Total	1,250	3,390	1,270	4,120	1,670	5,320

Source: House of Commons Hansard, 3 August 1978, Cols 271-6; and information supplied by DHSS.

- the numbers living below the official poverty line rose from 1,410,000 to 2,280,000.
- the numbers living at the SB level stood at 4,090,000 in 1976, a total which had risen from 3,730,000 two years earlier.
- the numbers living at an income up to 40 per cent above the SB poverty line was 5,260,000 in 1974 and had increased to 8,500,000 in 1976.

If we add these total together we find 14,870,000 people living in or around the margins of poverty in 1976. For reasons we explained earlier, this total probably underestimates the numbers of the very poor. Even so it equals a quarter of the population and tells us one very important fact about the distribution of income in our society and the Labour Government's failure to bring about the irreversible shift in resources to working people to which the Party was committed by the 1973 conference, or, more modestly, to "strike at the roots of the worst poverty" as was promised in the February 1974 Election Manifesto.

REDUCING THE NUMBERS ON MEANSTESTS

One of the longest established of Labour's social policy commitments has been the pledge to reduce the numbers of people dependent on meanstests. The Party went to the country in both the 1974 general elections with policies which were aimed to achieve just this.

There are six meanstested benefits which form a major part of our social security system. Were the numbers of people dependent on these benefits reduced during Labour's time in government, or did they grow in importance as Labour failed to implement its election pledges to poorer people?

Supplementary benefits

In 1964 Labour was committed to introducing a minimum guaranteed income free of meanstests to replace the National Assistance Scheme. The Wilson Government failed to honour this election pledge and, instead, replaced in 1966 the National Assistance Board with the supplementary benefit scheme. While some academics have been able to describe the major differences between the two schemes, claimants are of another opinion. The essential fact about both schemes is that benefit is only awarded after the recipient has submitted to a meanstest.

When the NAB was established in 1948 it was designed as the safety net in the welfare state. Moreover, it was planned that, as the population built up their contributory rights to national insurance benefits, the numbers needing to claim national assistance would fall. Indeed, Beveridge believed that, over time, the NAB would wither away.

This has not happened for two reasons. First, the national insurance benefits, such as old age pensions, were never paid at a generous enough level to guarantee working people an income above the poverty line when their benefit became their main, and often only, source of income. And a second Beveridge principle — that of benefit being paid for as long as need lasted — was also torpedoed. For example, the original scheme envisaged the payment of unemployment benefit for as long as a person was unemployed, was registered for work and had not refused with good reason jobs offered to him. Flat rate unemployment benefit is paid for the first twelve months to claimants with full contribution records, and the earnings related supplement for only the first six months of joblessness.

How effective was Labour in implementing its programme to reduce the numbers dependent on supplementary benefit? In 1974 there were 2,680,000 regular SB payments made. By 1979 this total had risen to 2,929,000. And while the number of payments to pensioners fell from a total of 1,712,000 to 1,628,000 (largely due to their transference to the rent and rate rebate scheme) the number of regular payments to heads of households below pensionable age grew from 872,000 in 1974 to 1,198,000 in 1978. Not surprisingly it was the increase in unemployment which contributed most to the swelling of the ranks of the poor.

The Family Income Supplement

The FIS scheme was introduced in 1971 against the full sound and fury of the Labour Opposition. In 1970 the Conservatives promised to increase family allowances if they won the election. Win they did, but family allowances (now child benefits) remained unchanged. Instead a new meanstested benefit was introduced for the poor in work who were responsible for bringing up children. As with all meanstests, the introduction of FIS was accompanied by the assurance that it was only a temporary measure, and as with all temporary meanstested benefits, FIS has taken on all the signs of living to a ripe old age. The numbers of poor working parents dependent on FIS since 1974 rose from 70,000 to 89,000 in 1977 (the latest data).

Rent and rate rebates

It was also the Heath Government that introduced the national rent and rebate scheme in 1972. While on the one hand rents were to be raised until they reached what was called a "fair" level, on the other, a national rebate scheme was introduced for those whose income was insufficient for them to meet the fair rent. When the national scheme came into operation in 1973 so the numbers claiming rebates increased two and a half times to 700,000. The national scheme was accompanied by a rent allowance scheme for tenants in private unfurnished accommodation, and just under 50,000 allowances were paid in 1973. Private furnished tenants were originally excluded from the scheme but were included a year later due to great pressure on the Government.

A national rate rebate scheme has existed since 1966 but it was not until 1975 that its and the rent rebate eligibility levels were unified. Since the introduction of the national scheme the numbers claiming rate rebates have increased enormously, the most substantial increase coming in 1975 when the income qualifying levels were raised from an absurdly low level to equal those for the rent rebate scheme. This accounts for much of the increase from 910,000 claimants in 1974 to 2,300,000 claimants a year later. But, in the absence of Labour reforming the rating system the numbers claiming rate rebates continued to climb and stood at 2,705,000 in 1978.

The numbers claiming rent rebates stood at 840,000 in 1974 and rose 985,000 by 1978. Claims for a rent allowance rose over the same period from 132,000 to 209,000.

Benefits for Children

There are two major meanstested benefits for children whose parents are poor; free welfare foods and free school meals. The number of children who qualified and claimed free welfare foods on the grounds of their parents' poverty stood at 318,000 in 1974 and rose to 388,000 in 1976 (latest data). With the Labour Government's phasing out of the school dinner subsidy, the number of families made eligible for free school meals was increased considerably. In 1974 three-quarters of a million children claimed free school meals. This total rose to 1,159,000 in 1978.

Increasing importance of meanstests under Labour

One message is clear and this is that many more people were dependent on meanstested assistance at the end of the 1974 Labour Government's rule than at the beginning. Part of the reason for this surge in the numbers on meanstests was that the eligibility levels for benefit were raised (as measured against average earnings). But such changes occurred because the Government was also embarking on other policies — such as the phasing out of subsidies — which hit at working families, and the political fig-leaf for such changes was to announce that the poor would not be hurt as the eligibility for means-tested assistance was being made more generous. Moreover, the Government failed to introduce other long promised reforms such as that of the rating system. To substitute a progressive local tax for the present rating system would have resulted in fewer, rather than more people being dependent on meanstested relief at the end of the Government's life compared to the numbers eking out an existence with the help of this type of support in 1974.

NARROWING THE GAP BETWEEN RICH AND POOR

Labour's October 1974 Manifesto spoke of the "real increase (in benefit) which more than compensates for the rise in prices". But was this real increase maintained?

The key information for any consideration of Labour's record to the poor is what happened to the relative value of supplementary benefit payments. Was the gap between the living standards of the poor and those on average earnings narrowed, and was this higher relative value maintained throughout the Government's life?

There are two ways of measuring the value of SB rates against average earnings: to take gross earnings as the base or to use net earnings i.e. after stoppages. The burden of taxation increased in two directions under the 1974/9 Labour Government. As we will see in the following section, it shifted horizontally onto families, irrespective of their level of income. And at the same time there occurred a vertical shift in the impact of taxation which increased not only the amount of tax paid by those on low incomes, but brought other low income earners into the tax net for the first time. One example will suffice to show this trend. In 1973/4 a married couple with two children did not begin to pay tax until their income rose above 51.3 per cent of average earnings. By 1978/9 they began to pay income tax as soon as their income increased beyond 43.8 per cent of average earnings.

Because the Government brought about this vertical shift in the burden of taxation, its record looks much more favourable if the relative value of benefits is measured against net earnings. If gross earnings are used little improvement occurred. But on a net earnings basis the SB rates for all forms of households increased in the years up to 1977. For example, for a single person the ordinary scale rate rose from 25.1 per cent of net average earnings in October 1973 to 29.3 per cent in November 1977, falling to 26.8 per cent a year later. A similar pattern occurs for claimants on the ordinary as well as the long term rate, except that for single claimants, married couples with small families, the fall in the value of the long term SB rates is far less marked. The single person's rate rose from 28.6 per cent of net average earnings in October 1973 to 36.1 per cent in November 1977, falling back to 34.4 per cent a year later. However, the fall for a four child family amounted to 7 percentage points (benefit valued at 76.5 per cent of net average earnings in 1977 and collapsing to 69.5 per cent in November 1978).

These figures do more than show that the Labour Government failed to maintain the relative improvement in living standards of the poor which it marked up in its earlier years, even when measured on the most favourable basis. They also show that long term beneficiaries fared better than those on the ordinary scale rate. And here it is important to remember that no matter how long an unemployed claimant has been on benefit, he and his family can never qualify for the long term rate. That the relative value of the ordinary rates fell much more drastically than the long term rates effectively discriminated against the unemployed. Similarly, the relative value of long term rates for larger families fell much more appreciably than for the childless and those with small families. And while the majority of poor families are small, poverty is more acute amongst those poor families with a larger number of children. Labour's benefit record therefore shows a discrimination against some of the very poorest families.

HELP FOR CHILDREN

Prior to the introduction of the child benefit scheme in 1977 there were two main forms of support for working families with children. Family allowances were paid to second and subsequent children and tax allowances were granted for each child, and varied according to their age. However, some of the poorest families only had one child, and therefore gained no help from family allowances, while others did not earn enough to claim the value of the child tax allowances (CTAs). Pressure began to mount for the merging of the two forms of support and for the payment of a universal cash allowance to mothers.

The promise

The promise to introduce this new benefit was in both of Labour's 1974 election manifestos. The need for this new benefit, together with a major injection of additional financial help to families, can be seen if we look at what had been happening to the net disposable income of different types of households in the years up to the advent of the 1974 Labour Government.

The group experiencing the greatest increase in net disposable income in the years from 1962 until the advent of the 1974 Labour Government were pensioners (although it must be said that their incomes rose from a very low level). Net disposable income for the single pensioner rose to 176 (1962 equal 100) and for a married couple it increased to 171. In contrast, the net disposable income of a two child family had risen only to 139.

This is not the place to recall the political manoeuvres associated with the near non-introduction of the child benefit scheme. Because of the leak of Cabinet papers on the scheme which I was given, we do know more about the way groups within the Party go about vetoing commitments (see *New Society* article, 17 June 1976) and this will be commented upon in the concluding section of this chapter.

What is relevant is to recall that the leak played a major part in ensuring that the government introduced the scheme in a very minor form and, more importantly, in mobilising a campaign for a major transference of funds to child support. (An outline of this campaign is given in Frank Field, "Last Word", *Social Work Today*, 2 May 1978.) The extent of this new outlay amounted to £700m in 1978 and an additional £1bn in 1979.

One part of the child benefit scheme is for the phasing out of child tax allowances and for the revenue thereby saved to be paid to mothers in a cash payment. Any consideration of the effectiveness of Labour's record therefore requires a twofold analysis. First, was the value of the child benefits when Labour left office greater than the combined value of CTAs and family allowances in 1974? Second, as child benefit also carries out the same role as CTAs in setting the tax free income of families, did the new benefit reverse the discrimination in the tax system from which families had suffered over the past fifteen years or so?

Value of child support

Table 4 presents the value of child support for selected years since 1946/7. For periods prior to 1971/2 the peak years have been selected

Table 4: Value of the child tax allowance and family allowance/child benefit as a percentage of gross earnings of manual workers

Married couple with	April 1955	April 1970	April 1971	April 1972	April 1973	April 1974	April 1975	April 1976	April 1977	April 1978	April 1979
1 child under 11	3.91	2.54	2.96	2.78	2.53	2.90	2.54	2.66	2.56	3.05	3.84
2 children under 11	4.53	2.93	3.36	3.16	2.85	3.17	3.03	3.07	2.75	3.05	3.84
3 children under 11	4.75	3.13	3.55	3.34	3.00	3.30	3.19	3.21	2.81	3.05	3.84
4 children under 11	4.85	3.23	3.64	3.43	3.08	3.36	3.27	3.28	2.84	3.05	3.84
1 child 11-15	—	—	3.42	3.22	2.99	3.34	2.90	2.97	2.82	3.29	3.84
2 children 11-15	—	—	3.83	3.60	3.30	3.59	3.40	3.38	3.00	3.29	3.84
3 children 11-15	—	—	4.02	3.78	3.45	3.72	3.56	3.52	3.07	3.29	3.84
4 children 11-15	—	—	4.12	3.87	3.52	3.78	3.64	3.59	3.10	3.29	3.84
1 child 16 plus	—	—	3.90	3.67	3.36	3.70	3.22	3.25	3.04	3.49	3.84
2 children 16 plus	—	—	4.30	4.04	3.67	3.95	3.71	3.65	3.22	3.49	3.84
3 children 16 plus	—	—	4.49	4.22	3.82	4.08	3.87	3.79	3.29	3.49	3.84
4 children 16 plus	—	—	4.64	4.36	3.91	4.15	3.96	3.86	3.22	3.49	3.32

The April 1979 child benefit rates have been deflated to November 1978 prices to reflect a year-on-year inflation rate of 8.5 per cent, for April 1979. This figure is in line with the Industry Act forecast published in the November 1978 Economic Progress Report.

Source: *Hansard* Vol.961, Cos 525-6, 1 February 1979.

so that Labour's record can be put into a longer perspective. But it is important to recall that even the best years show a level of financial support to families well below most of the other EEC members (see, for example, *Hansard,* 23 May 1979) and that the level of support for families has always been far from adequate, even in the most favourable years.

Taking the years since 1974 first we can see that, on leaving office, the Government's record was not a great deal better than when it came to power. Moreover, the level of financial support to families was substantially below the level provided in 1955/6.

Tax burden on families

Given the discrimination families faced in the tax/ benefit field in the years preceding 1974, how effective was the Labour Government in reversing this trend? Two sets of information show that the answer was that the discrimination was not reversed. Table 5 shows that in terms of tax-free income enjoyed by different household groups, families with children still continued to lose out. Similarly Table 6, which details the increases in the percentage of income paid in tax and national insurance, again demonstrates how families with children were asked to contribute the lion's share of the increase in the tax burden occurring under the Labour Government. Even worse, it was families on and below average earnings who suffered the largest cuts in their net disposable income. It is no wonder then that some politicians

Table 5: Tax free income in real terms, 1974-1979

April	Single person Money	real	Married couple Money	real	Married couple, 1 child Money	real	Married couple, 2 children Money	real	Married couple, 4 children Money	real
1974	100	100	100	100	100	100	100	100	100	100
1975	108	89	110	91	108	89	107	88	105	87
1976	118	81	125	87	125	87	126	87	127	88
1977	151	89	168	99	154	91	151	89	146	86
1978	158	86	177	97	159	87	153	88	144	78
1979	169	86	190	97	168	85	159	81	147	75

All children aged under 11 except in the four child family where one child is between the ages of 11 and 16.

Tax free income is income which can be received (including FAM or CB) without being liable to tax. Until 1976 includes clawback.

Inflation April 1978 to April 1979 is assumed to be 7% and personal allowances (excluding child allowances) increased by this amount.

CTA and Child Benefit figures for April 1979 are those already announced (CB −£4; CTA abolished for under 11; £35 for 11-16).

Table 6: Increases in the percentage of income paid in tax and national insurance contributions, 1978/9 compared with 1964/5

Household	2/3 average earnings	average earnings	Income 2 x average earnings	5 x average earnings	10 x average earnings
Single	54.1	36.0	26.6	69.6	64.7
Married couple	76.1	51.4	30.5	68.9	65.2
Married couple and 2 children	185.9	144.3	56.1	76.1	70.1

Source: Reworked from data given in a Parliamentary Answer to Mr Cranley Onslow, *House of Commons Hansard*, Vol.959, 1 December 1978, Cols 438-9.

found it easy to run the social security scares which scarred most of the years of this decade, but particularly those since 1974.

CONCLUSION

One of Labour's most important achievements was a rise in the real value of pensions and other long-term national insurance benefits. The impetus and sustaining power for this achievement came from the Trade Union Movement. Such interest was not shown by the Movement in other areas of social policy and the lesson is clear for reformers wishing to see the next Labour Government committed to a radical attack on poverty.

Left to its own devices the 1974/9 Labour Government failed in four important areas to live up to its election promises. The numbers of poor grew rapidly and particularly the numbers living below the SB poverty line. And with the rapid rise in the numbers of unemployed (up from 600,000 to 1,400,000 over the same period) the increase in poverty cannot be explained away on the grounds that a more generous definition of poverty has been adopted.

The steady increase in the numbers dependent on meanstested assistance was brought about by two failures in government policy.

The provision of a new non-meanstested benefit for families was vetoed by nothing short of trickery by leading ministers. The Cabinet were told that there was opposition amongst MPs to the introduction of the new child benefit scheme. This opposition turned out to be no more than a

THE POOR

belief by the Whips that backbenchers would be opposed to fulfilling this election pledge to families. Trade union leaders were then told of backbench opposition and great emphasis was placed on the switch of child tax allowances from fathers' wage packets to a cash benefit for mothers. Labour's commitment to child benefits was fulfilled only after these manoeuvres were made public. The case for more open government was forceably demonstrated as the supposedly powerful arguments for postponing indefinitely the introduction of the child benefit scheme melted away under the gaze of public debate.

The failure to implement child benefits at the beginning of the Parliament led to an increase in the numbers of families pushed onto meanstested assistance. Likewise, because family income was not adequately protected by generous child benefits, the run down of subsidies led to price increases (such as with school dinners, fuel prices and so on) which many working and poor families could not meet. The Government's response was to make more and more people eligible for one form or another of meanstested relief. Failure to protect the social wage therefore triggered off another failure as the Government was 'forced' to push more and more people onto meanstested benefits.

Labour's aim to improve the relative income of the poor was successful during the early part of the Parliament. But the failure to hold to the Party's economic policy resulted in a spill-over effect into other areas. Most of the relative gains in the living standards of the poor were wiped out in 1978. And those who gained least, and suffered most, were the unemployed and families with larger than average numbers of children.

Labour was similarly unsuccessful in bringing about a horizontal shift in the distribution of income. Despite a record injection of funds into the child benefit scheme, the value of family support at the end of the Government's life was less than that given to some families in 1971 let alone the peak year of 1955. The tax burden of families rose faster than for other groups and rose doubly fast for families on low incomes.

These failures cannot be explained away entirely by the collapse of the 1974/9 Labour Government's economic strategy. The lack of a clear grasp by Parliamentary leaders of the key role social policies have in an all out attack on poverty and inequality also played an important part.

VIII

Working Relations Between Government and Party*

Geoff Bish

Over the past five years, working through a network of sub-committees and study groups, the Home Policy Committee has been responsible for the publication of no less than 70 major NEC statements of one kind or another, including statements to Conference, the 60,000 word *Labour's Programme 1976,* evidence to Royal Commissions and direct submissions to the Labour Government itself. Over 2,000 research papers have been prepared, either within the Research Department or by outside experts: and resolutions from Annual Conferences — and from affiliated organisations in between Conferences — have been assiduously fed in to this extensive policy-making process.

In undertaking this arduous programme, the Committee has had two main objectives: first, to influence and shape the work of our own Labour Government; second, to provide a detailed, well-researched basis for our Manifesto, so that the

*Extract from paper on future programme of research work, presented to the Home Policy Committee of the Labour Party's National Executive Committee.

latter would accurately reflect the views and priorities of the Party. In the event, it is suggested, the NEC had scant success on either count: and the Committee might perhaps wish to reflect a little on why this was so. Among the problems associated with our policy work, for example, have been the following:

i. The status of the NEC and the Party, vis-à-vis the Cabinet: Despite all our efforts to prepare careful and detailed proposals, the status of the NEC vis-à-vis the Labour Government was, in practice, that of a mere pressure group, just one among many. The outcome of our numerous delegations, representations, statements and resolutions was thus little different from those of many other pressure groups: a few minor successes, perhaps, but little of real substance in the way of changing the *direction* of Government policy.

ii. The lack of involvement of the Cabinet in Party policy-making: Although Ministers were heavily represented on our sub-committees and study groups, this did not mean that the Government became committed in any way to the policies which emerged. There was certainly no real sense of *joint* decision-making. Indeed, apart from the Ministers directly 'involved', the Government displayed little serious interest in the policy-making effort of the NEC and the Party — except, that is, on occasion, to repudiate publicly certain of the proposals put forward. (Labour's Programme, for example, was never considered or discussed by the Cabinet, or seen by the Govern-

GOVERNMENT AND PARTY

ment as a serious contribution to the debate about strategy.) Clearly, in all of this there were faults on both sides: but we surely cannot afford as a Party to continue to prepare our policies in this way.

iii. The lack of involvement by the Party in Government decision-making: The Labour Government's practice of issuing consultation documents in advance of proposals for legislation — and the various other initiatives on consultation — did help to open up a little the process of decision-making in Government. In the main, however, there was little effective *advance* consultation by the Government with the NEC, especially about major policy developments; and certainly seldom — if ever — on a basis of trying to reach agreed, joint decisions on what should be done. In many cases, indeed, the NEC was at a disadvantage compared to other major interest groups, including the CBI, the City, the TUC and others.

iv. The procedure for drawing up the Manifesto: At an early stage last year, the NEC agreed that the Manifesto should be drawn up in a careful, unhurried manner, well in advance of the calling of the election: and that the Manifesto itself should reflect as far as possible the considered, detailed policies of the NEC and Conference. No less than eight NEC-Cabinet Working Groups were set up to agree as much of the content as possible: and on the basis of this work — but with established Party policy clearly in mind — a first draft was prepared by the office. This draft was then considered paragraph by paragraph by a further NEC-Cabinet group (which held eleven meetings in all); and further agreements were concluded. After all this, however, it was the hurried and incomplete draft prepared by No.10 which became the basis of the Manifesto — a draft which not only ignored many of the agreed decisions of the NEC-Cabinet Group, but also many basic planks of Party policy. Indeed, the draft, as hastily amended by a drafting committee, was first seen by the NEC on the very day the Manifesto was to be presented to the Press.

v. Lack of consultation with Party members in the development of NEC policy: In the *preparation* of its detailed statements, the NEC has relied heavily on the relatively small number of researchers, backbenchers, trade unionists, academics and the like who serve on the advisory sub-committees. With the exception of the rural areas study, no procedures have been devised to provide for systematic consultation within the Party *before* statements are issued as policy. Neither have we been able to provide properly for political education within the Party about the new policies whilst they were still under discussion. As a result, we have failed to build up either the support or the understanding we need, within the Party, to help carry our policies through into the Manifesto and Government action.

vi. The status of NEC statements and the procedure for endorsement: In the process of *endorsing* NEC policy, Conference has all too often been expected to adopt — without amendment and with minimal debate — lengthy documents, even though these documents might have been circulated far too late for proper discussion and decision by affiliated organisations, prior to Conference. In the case of the numerous NEC statements issued between Conference, moreover, Conference is not consulted at all. (The NEC Report to Conference merely *lists* these statements. It is thus not clear whether or not they are to be considered as part of Labour's Programme — under Clause V — and thus count as essential raw material for the Manifesto — a question frequently asked about our statement on animal welfare.) These weaknesses in procedure have again helped to undermine both the status of our policies and the degree of commitment to them felt by affiliates and members.

Whilst it is only sensible for the Committee to bear these issues in mind when discussing its programme of work, they clearly range beyond the province of the Home Policy Committee alone. The Committee might wish, therefore, to consider asking the NEC to set up a small working group on 'Policy Development with the Party'; or, alternatively, to request the present Enquiry Committee to establish a small group. In either case, it would seem appropriate to include within the membership of such a group the chairmen of the Home Policy, International, Organisation and Press and Publicity Committees.

Even at this stage, however, some preliminary conclusions might be drawn from the lessons learnt from the past five years:

First, we need to consult much more widely in the Party before coming to firm policy conclusions.

One way of doing this might be to issue our policy statements, wherever possible, in *draft* form, for discussion and comment by affiliates, interested organisations and experts. Admittedly, this will not be possible for some items — such as evidence to Royal Commission and the like — given the tight deadlines to which we sometimes have to work. But the 'green paper' format, it is suggested, should become the norm — preferably published as a short consultation document, accompanied by more detailed background material.

A sustained effort, however, should then be made to ensure that local parties and affiliates do actually respond: through the calling, for example, of specialised regional conferences; through the political education programme (Politics 79 and Discussion Papers); and through *Labour Weekly* and the proposed new Party Journal. A report could then be made available to the NEC on the outcome of these consultations, together with the observations of other interested parties, such as the TUC or Labour Party specialists — and also giving the views of the Parliamentary Labour Party (PLP) and the Shadow Cabinet.

Second, arising from the above, we should perhaps in future not try to aim for an NEC endorsement for every line and comma of detailed policy statements. This is not to say that the NEC should not do its homework on a particular issue, or that the detail should not be ready to hand. But the full commitment of the NEC could perhaps be limited only to the basic outline of the policy, together with particularly important points of detail.

Third, we need to ensure that the PLP — and especially the PLP leadership — are not only more closely involved that hitherto in our policy-making, but also that they become much more *committed* to the policies as they emerge. This could mean, for example, seeking to resolve serious differences of view between the NEC and Shadow spokesmen through proper NEC/Shadow Cabinet discussion — and joint decision — in the light of Conference decisions. (Tony Benn's proposal for monthly NEC/Shadow Cabinet meetings, possibly as a small standing joint committee, could be the way ahead here.) But we could also try to liaise more closely with the PLP in other ways — for example, by sending them copies of resolutions received from our affiliates; and by asking for formal comments from the PLP on the draft statements proposed above.

IX

Whitehall's Short Way With Democracy

Michael Meacher, MP

One of the things that went wrong, badly wrong, for the Government was the actual process of government itself.

There is a convenient and widely held view of the British Constitution that Governments are elected to power and then, assisted by an impartial civil service, proceed to implement the policies on which they were elected. The truth is very different. And it is important that the truth be known because unless the real nature of the exercise of power in Whitehall is publicly understood, the abuse of power and obstruction of democracy that constantly occurs will not be identified and therefore not remedied.

There are five main ways in which the civil service subverts the effect of the democratic vote. It is not conspiratorially but because of the conservatism of the machine, because the training of civil servants is directed towards being critical of ideas rather than constructive and because the whole apparatus of Whitehall is tied to the consensus. One is the manipulation of individual Ministers, an exercise in man-management which is skilfully

DEMOCRACY AND WHITEHALL

orchestrated and on which a great deal of time and care is spent in the cause of 'Whitehall knows best'. Second is the isolation of Ministers and the resulting dependence on the Whitehall machine, for which a heavy price in policy terms is paid. Third is the exploitation of the inter-departmental framework, in order to circumvent Ministers who may be opposing the Whitehall consensus. Fourthly there is the close inter-lock with Establishment interests outside, which often means officials are acting in concert with the extra-Parliamentary power structure against Ministers rather than in support of the political Manifesto of the governing party. A fifth factor is the selective restriction on the dissemination of information, which keeps the power of decision-making limited in fewer hands and rebuts undesired Ministerial or public intrusion, especially into the most sensitive areas of policy. Each of these five main devices needs to be spelt out in detail.

The first is the Whitehall technique of managing Ministers. It takes many forms. A chief means is the filtering of information by officials. Papers are progressively screened out as they proceed upwards through the civil service hierarchy, and in contentious issues the 'line' will be decided by the top official, the Permanent Secretary. Thereafter, in subsequent meetings with the Minister, other officials will not demur or support the Minister against the official 'line', even if they had put strong counter-arguments previously, and the alternatives to the accepted line may not even be put forward because promotion prospects, future postings and future quality of work depend on the support of senior officials. Indeed, once when officials *did* put up alternative proposals open-endedly for Ministerial choice, the Permanent Secretary reprimanded them and insisted that the Departmental preference should be clearly argued for in future. Sometimes the impression is given that the aim is not so much to offer the Minister helpful and impartial advice as to browbeat him into submission: I have witnessed meetings where a dozen officials file in to deliver the Minister, whatever may be their private views, a sustained and obediently orchestrated attack on his policy line.

Or relevant information may be simply withheld from Ministers partly on the grounds, no doubt that Ministers may have limited time to read papers. Forecasts of economic trends, for example in the case of unemployment, might be 'doctored', and if forecasts would not be 'acceptable' to a senior Minister as being too disturbing, they might not be shown to him, lest otherwise he be diverted from unpopular policies. Again, information might be withheld simply to make life easier for civil servants. Thus an official reported to me, after a Minister had expressed interest in a certain policy area, that his Under-Secretary told him when he proposed to let the Minister have some data: "No. Don't bother. It might set a precedent. I'd get complaints from the others (officials)". Information is decidely not made available spontaneously to assist a Minister's known views where these diverge from officials' preconceptions. As one official remarked after a strained meeting with a Minister, "That went well — I didn't tell him anything he wanted to know".

Equally, the *timing* of the delivery of information to Ministers is crucial, and is played to advantage by the civil service. This may be blatant, as when officials once privately confided about a particular Minister: "He causes trouble, so we put in the papers late to him". Or it may be done more subtly. A large Cabinet Office position paper, of perhaps 10-50 pages, which officials had been mulling over for months, might be put into the Minister's night box for his approval for a meeting next morning. The Minister might come upon this long, detailed and complicated document for the first time after midnight, and have no more time than to glance through it, concentrating on the conclusions. Yet if the document were passed the next day, the whole of it, which most or even all Ministers had not properly read and certainly not thought through in depth, became 'the agreed policy of the government'.

Even if overwhelming a Minister with rushed paper-work is the most notorious method of harnessing Ministers to Whitehall-chosen priorities, it is not the only way of securing co-operation. A more insidious technique is the regular (though informal) confidential Whitehall briefing of the press about the Minister's performance. A compliant Minister will get good private reporting. An independent-minded one, who insists on his Party's Manifesto commitments against the advice of the mandarins, risks a formidable barrage of vilification directed against him in the press aided and abetted by civil servants. The stabbing in the back of Tony Benn for his championship of Labour's industrial policy and of Barbara Castle over phasing out pay beds in the NHS were two main examples in the last Labour Government. Some of the material for these press campaigns came from senior officials, like the leaking of the Accounting Officer minute in 1975 sent by Peter Carey to Tony Benn, which was designed to show that the latter's support for industrial co-operatives was somehow constitutionally improper.

A second way in which civil service practice undermines the effect of democratic choice is to exploit Ministers' isolation and dependence on the Whitehall machine. As Lord Armstrong, former Head of the Civil Service, has said: "The biggest and most pervasive influence is in setting the framework within which questions of policy are raised . . . It would have been enormously difficult for any Minister to change the framework, and to that extent we had great power". Officials retain the 'power of the drafter'. It's not that draft papers can't always be amended by Ministers — of course they can be provided Ministers have time to do so — but rather that much undoubtedly slips through which, written by officials with particular Departmental prejudices, would never have been *initiated* by Ministers in this form. Drafting of papers almost always starts off without prior consultation — oral or otherwise — with Ministers, so that by the time the papers reach them they are usually too late and in too final form for much Ministerial input to be introduced. More insidiously however, much that Ministers probably *would* have initiated themselves lies dormant in that, given the never-ending pressure of paper and meetings, they tend only to *react*.

So far from responding as passive recipients of Ministerial initiatives, Departments actually wage a sustained and sometimes aggressive campaign to recruit the Minister to *their* own way of thinking. Each Department has its own traditional policy doctrines, and it requires a very determined and persistent Minister to change them. Any new Ministerial inputs outside this Whitehall consensus encounter sharp resistance, with every possible objection put forward, many of them fairly trivial or destructive. No attempt is usually made by officials to be helpful in suggesting how these objectives might best be overcome or how an alternative course of action might better lead in the Minister's desired direction.

On the contrary, Ministers are regarded in Whitehall essentially as spokesmen for their Departments. So far from being seen as the political guardians of their Party Manifesto, they are ranked in Whitehall and the media according to how well they do for their Departments. Thus a Defence Minister is not hailed if he cuts defence expenditure as he is electorally pledged, but by how well he protects, or preferably increases, his Department's budget. There is a very strong predisposition in Whitehall that the role for Ministers is to wait for officials to come to decisions on policy issues and then be briefed on what to say in public presentation of the line worked out.

Part and parcel of this attitude is the open Whitehall deference towards Ministers to their faces, but a thinly veiled condescending arrogance behind the scenes. "Oh, there's no point in telling Ministers that — they won't understand it". "If anything could be done, don't you think that we would have thought of it?" Indeed, a common view is that Ministers are rather interfering and distract officials from getting on with schemes they already themselves have under way.

But perhaps the most serious form of exposure to dependence on Whitehall lies in the obligation on a Minister to work through a Permanent Secretary and senior officials whom he did not choose (and, in some cases, certainly never would have chosen) and who may have determinedly different political views about objectives or priorities. And it is exceedingly hard to remove such a person (though John Silkin's influence led to Freddie Kearns' departure from MAFF, Barbara Castle failed to remove Thomas Padmore from the Ministry of Transport when all the other Parliament Secretaries threatened to resign if she persisted).

A third way in which Whitehall subverts the democratic process lies in the ruthless use that is made of the inter-departmental network to circumvent an awkward Minister. One device here is for civil servants who face a Minister holding out against them to contact their opposite numbers in other Departments and brief them as to how they should brief *their* Ministers to oppose their own

Minister in the inter-departmental Ministerial committee discussing the issue. More regularly but less overtly by the seniority and strength of official representation at inter-departmental meetings, other departments can be given the lead as to how to play their hand or be shown if the heart of the department's officials is really in the fight. Other departments can then be given 'indications' as to how they should brief their Ministers. Or where a Minister seeks to consult outside pressure groups in advance of a government decision on an important issue (and where therefore the consultation could itself lead to pressure influencing the decision), his officials, where they oppose this move, may retail this intention to colleagues in the Cabinet Office or Treasury and thus secure the thwarting, by intervention from other Departments, of any such opening up of the Whitehall game to outsiders.

Again the committee network may be manipulated to keep out the relevant Minister. Thus in 1975 major industrial issues were examined first by the Industrial Development Unit, an in-house investigatory unit in DOI, then passed to the Industrial Development Advisory Board, an outside committee of businessmen, financiers, etc., and then it was proposed they should go to IDV(O), the official-level Industrial Development inter-departmental committee, and then to IDV, the Ministerial-level Industrial Development inter-departmental committee, before the relevant Minister, the Secretary of State for Industry, was given the full facts and an opportunity to comment.

Similarly, special ad hoc committees may be set up to outflank the relevant Minister's control. Recent examples include the CPRS study of the motor car industry, a Treasury-chaired inter-departmental committee on the steel industry, and an external group of 'wise men', the Ryder committee, on BLMC.

Perhaps the most insidious use of inter-departmental committees, however, is simply to get unwanted Ministerial initiatives lost. As an official once said: "In Whitehall we can co-ordinate anything into the ground". Officials' deliberate procrastination can take several forms — saying that there is another committee sitting on this or a related area, so one must wait for their report; or that officials should consider the proposal first and then they take a very long time to report (hoping the Minister in the meantime will lost interest or be moved); or that the cost is too great and the Treasury won't wear it, etc.

Another way in which officials work together inter-departmentally to block an independent-minded Minister is their devaluation of his opposition through their letting it be known that this represents only his personal view. Thus one senior official told his own Minister that he should be able to handle interventions by the Foreign Secretary "who will almost certainly be speaking against the brief from his Department". Or again, "the Minister is advised to object to the proposal in para . . . which we understand was added at the last moment and against all advice by Mr (a Minister in another Department)". Or as another top official wrote to his Minister, pursuing the favourite Whitehall sport of anti-Bennery: "If you wish to upstage Mr Benn, . . ."

But even without these subterranean devices, the official committee bringing its inter-departmental cohesive view to bear on Ministers in a single official policy paper is a very powerful force. As Crossman said in his diaries: "I have yet to see a Minister prevail against an inter-departmental official paper without the backing of the Prime Minister, the First Secretary, or the Chancellor". And he went on, correctly, that: "though Cabinet Ministers have this enormous limitation on their power of decision-making, I am sure that non-Cabinet Ministers find it much more difficult to impose their views on their civil servants".

A fourth aspect of the Whitehall undermining of Parliamentary democracy lies in the enmeshing of the senior echelons of the civil service within the business-finance power structure outside. This occurs at both the administrative and personal levels.

Administratively, when Ministers ask for a brief on a particular issue, especially in the industrial and economic Departments, the source of the information provided by officials — and also of the interpretation placed on it — is invariably the CBI, top managements of individual companies, the Bank of England or particular finance houses. Naturally these bodies are a main source of economic data and forecasting, but more significantly it is *their* policy slant rather than that of any other group (since the TUC is not regularly consulted) which permeates the documents put before Ministers. The Industrial Strategy put before Ministers in mid-1975, for example, which recommended concentrating on profitable industries and not pressing too hard to prevent closures or the decline of certain industrial sectors, had long been urged by Department of Industry officials at the behest of the CBI.

Conversely, where Ministers pressed for a policy to which these outside interests were hostile, even though it was a policy explicitly foreshadowed in a Manifesto commitment, top officials refused to co-operate. Thus, when the last Labour Government's first White Paper on industrial policy was being drawn up in 1974, Department of Industry officials refused point blank to draft the section on the National Enterprise Board as being 'political'. Similarly, when the pay bed proposals were first mooted by Ministers in the DHSS in 1975, in accordance with their election commitment, the Permanent Secretary on behalf of the Departments, and reflecting the fierce opposition of consultants outside, refused to proceed. The Secretary of State, Barbara Castle, was obliged to send him a reply *ordering* him to prepare proposals to which her Party was committed.

At a more personal level the links between top officialdom and leading industrialists and financiers are very close. They dine together frequently at the Oxford and Cambridge University Club in Pall Mall and at other select clubs around Whitehall. It is senior officials who are in fact predominantly responsible (subject to Ministerial approval, which is generally forthcoming) for appointments to leading public sector posts on the now notorious quangos. And, conversely, it is senior officials who after their retirement at 60 from the civil service enjoy in so many cases the benefits of lucrative appointments in private industry.

Many illustrations could be given, but one good example is the Industrial Development Advisory Board set up to give advice to the Secretary of State for Industry on important questions of Government industrial aid. Of the 12 members, 11 in 1974 were company chairmen or senior directors (though this was later reduced to 9). On the other side, in the Commons debate on the civil service on 15 January this year, Brian Sedgemore quoted research which showed that no less than 26 top civil servants of Permanent Secretary or equivalent level who retired between 1974-77 had been recruited by firms in the private sector.

This close symbiotic relationship with leading representatives of industry and finance must inevitably raise questions of the impartiality of civil service advice. Not that any implication of conspiracy is intended here, but rather that similarity of class origin and mutuality of interest tends to lead the civil service to a view of what is right in any given situation which closely coincides with the Establishment consensus outside Whitehall.

How far this harmony of interest with industry and finance outside tempts senior civil servants is a matter for conjecture. But there are some pointers. John Pardoe as MP in November 1976 stated he had received reliable reports that a number of people from Britain representing both Treasury and City interests had at that time told the US Treasury that it would be better if Britain were to get no more loans from the IMF or the international financial community. On similar lines, Professor Fred Hirsch asserted in 1977 that the IMF was largely the vehicle by which domestic groups, including the City, Bank and Treasury, could get extra power behind their elbows to jog elected Ministers. This raises questions as to whether this is a valid way for Whitehall (or any other group) to increase its authority in order to secure unpopular decisions, or whether it is manipulation to obtain sacrifices from the people not otherwise obtainable whilst preserving Establishment authority intact.

Most striking of all perhaps here is the story by Joe Haines of the attempt in June 1975 by the Treasury and the Bank of England, by letting the pound slide down, to 'bounce' the Cabinet into statutory wage controls in defiance of Labour's repeated election pledges. Claiming that the Treasury did nothing to arrest the slump in the pound and used the crisis to force policies on the Labour Government which Business favoured, though these had already destroyed the Heath Government and had been totally repudiated by Labour, Haines describes this action as an attempted 'civilian coup against the Government'.

The fifth factor of Whitehall power, which operates more to secure the interests of the civil service than the democratic interests of the wider community, is the restrictive control exercised on the flow of information. Certainly it is true that a great deal of information is published by Government sources — indeed to the extent that one senior figure remarked, only half in jest, "If you give enough people enough information, nobody will know what's going on". But much important information is *not* published (quite apart from matters of national security or commercial confidentiality, which should obviously not be published), or is subject to such limited circulation in Whitehall as to affect the decisions finally taken.

One example is the way that Cabinet Office tightly controls the number of sets of Cabinet papers which are made available to Cabinet Ministers. These papers may arrive as late as 48 hours before the Cabinet meeting at which they are to be discussed. Previously, only three copies were provided, with instructions that they were not to be copied, but after the child benefit leak in June 1976 this was cut still further to two copies only. One set goes to the Permanent Secretary for the relevant official to prepare briefing. Thus only one other set of papers is available for the Minister's own use, which makes it unnecessarily difficult to arrange for other comments to be sought even from fellow Ministers.

Another revealing example of information handling lies in the Budget preparations. It is a working principle in Whitehall that the more important the decision, the fewer the people who have access to it. By contrast, the background data to some of the more trivial decisions that fall to Government is often disseminated widely and may be discussed at tedious length in Cabinet sub-committees, thus keeping Junior Ministers occupied with relevant minutiae. The Budget proposals, on the other hand, are kept very tightly restricted. Though they may dramatically influence a Department's strategy, even Cabinet Ministerial colleagues are only informed of the details 24 hours before public delivery. Similarly, other key Treasury decisions affecting overall economic strategy are not subjected to the same inter-departmental discussion as other issues are, but are confined essentially to a small élite group of official advisers round the Chancellor.

In general, information management is a skill highly developed in Whitehall. It can work both ways, both for the suppression of information which might be too sensitive a challenge to the official line and also for the elaborately prepared release so as to give the public impression that is officially desired.

On the former, a considerable range of information which is not strictly covered by security or commercial confidentiality criteria (e.g. the Government's medium-term economic assessment) is withheld, even from Parliamentary Questions. Moreover, data on embarrassing topics may be blocked (e.g. in 1976 the number of retired top civil servants who received a rise of more than £40 a week in inflation-proofed pensions, and at the other end of the scale the number of civil servants working for the Supplementary Benefits Commission on low enough wages to be entitled to Family Income Supplement). Or to give another illustration of how a controversial issue may be handled: when a Parliamentary Question was put down asking the number of licence applications received for the export of works of art from the Mentmore sale, the Departmental official concerned refused to give the number (which was very large) because, since the Treasury had refused help over the sale, it was necessary to protect colleagues from comeback. When told this breached the public entitlement to know and that secrecy here was unwarrantable, he replied "Well, this is certainly contrary to the rules of the game — the way it's normally played".

Equally, the release of information can be, and is, used to achieve certain political results and not simply to provide unbiassed factual material. One example here has been the exaggerated forecasts of the Public Sector Borrowing Requirement, designed indirectly to induce wage moderation. More generally, the whole system of private press briefings by senior officials or press departments within Ministries is designed to push the official line. Information released in support of the Whitehall consensus is 'briefing'; information released which challenges the consensus is a 'leak'. Briefings may be used not only to increase knowledge, but also at times to disguise the truth, to divert attention, to float ideas, to render what is big small, and to render trivial what is secretly enormous.

In short, the power system in Whitehall is in no sense a democracy, but rather a mandarin-dominated bureaucracy with only limited Ministerial control. If democracy is seriously intended, in the sense of electing a government with the effective power of enforcing its electoral pledges on the state officialdom, then this present power system requires a very radical overhaul. That task has now perhaps become more important than the preparation of any specific new policy departure since only if the former is tackled can the latter be expected to be achieved. That is the measure of what now needs to be done at the centre of government.

X

Drafting The Manifesto*

Geoff Bish

The Policy Background

In the years immediately preceding the 1979 election, the NEC and the Party had carried out an impressive and unprecedented range of studies and discussions on the policies which it wished to be considered for inclusion in the Manifesto:

First, Conference had, as early as 1976, considered and endorsed a comprehensive statement of policy, "Labour's Programme for Britain". And in commending this statement to Conference, the NEC made it clear that they saw it as providing the broad basis for the next Manifesto, as laid down in Clause V of the Party Constitution.

Second, Conference had subsequently endorsed a number of further statements and resolutions, thus providing still greater depth and precision to many of the sometimes vague commitments set out in Labour's Programme. And each statement was passed at Conference either on a two-thirds card vote or with little or no dissent. The subjects covered included:

*Extract from paper presented to the Home Policy Committee of the Labour Party's National Executive Committee.

Banking and Finance	The House of Lords
The EEC	The House of Commons
Construction	The Civil service
Race Relations	Freedom of Information
Multinationals	The Environment
The Arts	Local Government Reform

Third, the NEC had published a number of further major statements of policy, in between the Annual Conferences — often presented as evidence to official enquiries or Royal Commissions. The subjects covered ranged across the whole spectrum of domestic policy and they included:

Broadcasting and the Press	The NHS
Industrial Democracy	Immigration
Transport	Racial Discrimination
Education	Council Housing; and Council House Sales
Rents	Animal Welfare
Housing Finance	The Community Land Act
Legal Services	Agricultural Land
Economic Policy (Budget)	Local Authority Mortgage Lending

Fourth, the Party had already given serious advance consideration to which commitments from Labour's Programme it wished to see included in the Manifesto. Its views were set out in a special statement — a "campaign document" — presented by the NEC to the 1977 Conference, and carried overwhelmingly.

Fifth, the TUC, the Party and the Government had issued, through the tripartite Liaison Committee, a series of joint statements setting out the priorities for the immediate future. The 1978 version, "Into the Eighties", was endorsed by Conference and expected to provide a further important input to the Manifesto. But this was not all: for the Liaison Committee was also responsible for a number of further joint declarations in key areas of policy, such as child benefits and the wealth tax — declarations which left little scope for any lack of clarity on the policy.

And sixth, the NEC was able to draw upon the wealth of Party experience and expertise on its own sub-committees and study groups: and this expertise was extensively drawn upon by the NEC in preparing and clarifying its proposals for the Manifesto, right up to the point of preparing draft paragraphs for inclusion.

The Nature of the Manifesto

During the lifetime of the Labour Government numerous differences of view emerged between Ministers and NEC members on the meaning of important Manifesto commitments. Sometimes the commitment turned out to be too vague or unclear; sometimes Ministers preferred to interpret the commitment in their own way because of a basic lack of sympathy on their part with the proposal itself; or sometimes it was found that the commitment had not been properly thought through and could not be implemented without modification. But as a result of these difficulties, NEC members did become sharply aware of the need for the

Manifesto to be clear and unambiguous in its commitments — *and* for the proposals to have been properly worked out beforehand.

As we have seen earlier, the NEC took great care to ensure that its policies had been properly thought through and that they would stand up to the test of practicability. But in addition, the Executive also gave considerable thought to the *nature* of the Manifesto, to whether or not it would be possible to set out the commitments in sufficient detail to avoid confusion or doubt.

As early as July 27, 1978, therefore, a special meeting of the Home Policy Committee was held to consider these issues. The Committee agreed that:

"The Manifesto should be seen primarily as a programme of action, clear and unambiguous, for the next Government; *and this consideration should determine the length and nature of the Manifesto* . . . Wherever helpful, a cross-reference should be made to Labour Programme 1976 so that our policy commitments can be as clear as possible."

It was this approach that determined the nature not only of the early drafts of the Manifesto, but also of the various submissions from the NEC's own sub-committees and study groups, of the work of the joint NEC-Cabinet Working Groups (which laboured away during 1977 and 1978) and even of the high-level NEC-Cabinet Group which worked through the draft during the first three months of 1979. It was always accepted, of course, that that final version would have to be a good deal punchier than these early drafts. But it was also generally accepted that explicit commitments *would* be included — and in sufficient detail to leave no room for doubt on their meaning. It was a view, however, which did not survive the first few minutes of the final drafting committee set up by the NEC.

COUNT-DOWN TO THE MANIFESTO

The first stage: The Cabinet/NEC Working Groups

On February 16, 1977, the NEC and Cabinet discussed a paper entitled "An Agenda for Agreement". This paper prepared by myself after consultation with No.10, proposed the setting up of a number of small groups of NEC members and Cabinet Ministers whose purpose would be, initially, to try to bridge some of the huge differences of view between the two sides. At a later stage, it was suggested, the work of the group could be pulled together and published as a 'Campaign Document' — a forerunner to the Manifesto proper. (This two-stage procedure had been very successfully employed for the February 1974 election).

In the event, the Prime Minister and the Cabinet were not prepared to commit themselves at that stage to a Campaign Document; and only four groups were to be set up, on a 'pilot' basis — *Unemployment, Prices, Social Policy* (to include Education), and *Industrial Policy* (Economic Policy was explicitly excluded from the list of groups). As expected, it took a good deal of time and effort to get these groups under way, given the various problems of membership, the crowded diaries of Ministers, the Summer Recess, the Conference period, and the rest. Indeed, the groups did not begin meeting before *November 1977.*

The secretariat for the groups was on a joint basis: political advisors on the one hand, and Transport House researchers on the other. For each of the groups, the Research Department provided a basic policy brief drawn from Labour's Programme, Conference decisions and NEC Statements. Ministers and their Departments were then invited to respond — with the aim of trying to prepare jointly agreed drafts for report to an early meeting of the Cabinet and NEC.

In November 1977, a meeting of the Cabinet and NEC agreed to set up a similar group on the EEC, to discuss the NEC Statement to Conference, and the letter from the Prime Minister to the NEC. This group had its first meeting in March 1978.

In May 1978, at a meeting of the Campaign Committee, the Prime Minister agreed to extend the range of policy work covered by the groups. *By July 1978*, groups on Economic Policy, Housing (to include Land and Transport), and on the Machinery of Government, had begun to meet.

Although progress tended to be rather halting with these groups, they did help enormously to narrow down the areas of difference and, in some cases (such as on social, industrial and economic policy, on education, on machinery of government and on the EEC), substantial drafts were able to be agreed for inclusion in a first draft Manifesto.

THE MANIFESTO 193

The second stage: "Keep Britain Labour"

In July 1978, the office prepared for the NEC a "Progress Report" on the Manifesto. This document, discussed at a special meeting of the Home Policy Committee on July 27, set out the main policy commitments which, it suggested, should be included in the Manifesto: and it not only drew upon the work of the NEC/Cabinet Working Groups, but also included the "uncompleted business" of the 1974 Manifesto, the TUC-Labour Party joint Statements and Conference decisions. The document also suggested some of the important problems and issues to which the Manifesto ought to be addressed.

On September 11, 1978, the Home Policy Committee considered the first drafts from the NEC/Cabinet Working Groups, together with additional drafts from some of the NEC's own sub-committees. It agreed to instruct the office to prepare a draft "Campaign Document" — as "the basis for future manifesto consultations". It also agreed to call for a special meeting of the NEC to consider the draft and to seek "an extensive meeting" between the NEC and Cabinet to finalise a draft for publication. The Committee was particularly concerned to ensure that the NEC and the Cabinet did not have quickly to finalise a hurried Manifesto draft. Instead, a number of joint meetings should be held, with the publication of a Campaign Document preceding, if possible, the Manifesto itself.

At the November NEC, however, the Prime Minister proposed an early meeting between a small group of NEC members and some members of the Cabinet, be held in December, for "a preliminary discussion on issues and policies likely to be strong candidates for inclusion in a Manifesto". This was agreed — but subject to the proviso that it would in no way pre-empt the special meeting of the NEC on the Manifesto (this special meeting was never held).

On December 4, 1978, the Home Policy Committee considered the document 'NEC Proposals for the Manifesto' (Keep Britain Labour)*. This drew together the various drafts from the NEC-Cabinet Working Groups — and the drafts from the NEC's own sub-committees (where there was no appropriate joint group — such as with Local Government and Agriculture); and it also suggested some compromise draft paragraphs where sharp differences of view had emerged within the NEC/Cabinet groups. A number of amendments were agreed; and the office was asked to provide an amended draft. (The December NEC also discussed the draft but no definite conclusions or amendments emerged.)

Third stage: the NEC/Cabinet Working Group

On December 20, 1978, members of the NEC and the Cabinet met to decide how to proceed on the Manifesto. Although the NEC had originally expressed some opposition to this meeting turning itself into a Manifesto Working Group, this is what,

---

*A further meeting was held on December 12, to complete the discussion.

THE MANIFESTO

in effect, it became.* The group agreed to work through the NEC draft, section by section; to invite the appropriate Ministers and the Chairmen of NEC sub-committees as and when their section was being discussed; and that the secretariat would be provided jointly between Transport House and No.10. It was also agreed that the document would need to be reduced in length, especially in the various descriptive and analytical sections.

Between January and March 1979 the Group met on almost a weekly basis. It held eleven meetings in all; and the following policy areas were covered, at least in part:

Housing	Agriculture
Construction	Human Rights
Planning and Land	Race and Immigration
Education	The media
Youth	The arts
Social Security	Women's Rights
Health	Local Government
Transport	Industrial Democracy
Central Government (including the Lords and Open Government)	Energy

Admittedly, substantial differences remained to be resolved in each of these areas — and these were referred upwards to the full Cabinet/NEC meeting (the 'Clause V meeting'). But considerable progress was able to be made both at the meetings of the

---

*The Committee included the Officers and Chairmen of Committees of the NEC, plus two additional trade union representatives. The Cabinet side included the Deputy Leader and the Chancellor of the Exchequer.

Groups and via informal contacts between Transport House, the Ministers and the political advisors. And agreed texts did eventually emerge, albeit with various sentences or paragraphs still 'in square brackets'.

Fourth stage: the confidence vote and the aftermath

At the NEC on Wednesday March 28, it was agreed to hold a special meeting of the NEC before the "Clause V" Cabinet/NEC meeting, should the Government be defeated that afternoon. The Government was defeated: and the meeting was fixed for Monday, April 2, with a full NEC-Cabinet meeting on Friday, April 6. But a good deal happened in the meantime:

1. On Thursday, March 29 No.10 revealed to the General Secretary that it had already prepared a draft manifesto, based "to some extent" on the drafts agreed within the NEC-Cabinet Working Group.

2. The NEC had not, at that point, yet had sight of the various agreements which had been made in the NEC-Cabinet Working Group. It was therefore agreed to send out to the NEC, for its Monday meeting, a complete set of the Minutes of the NEC-Cabinet Group.

3. The NEC had not yet considered *any* of the items left outstanding by the NEC-Cabinet Group. These included not only the various "square bracketed" paragraphs left over from the previous discussions, but also the critical

THE MANIFESTO

area of economic, fiscal and industrial policy which had not been touched by the Group.

4. Late on Friday March 30, the Research Secretary first had sight of the No.10 draft. It was, in his view, appalling. Not only did it ignore entire chapters of Party policy: it overturned and ignored many of the agreements which had been laboriously hammered out within the NEC-Cabinet Group.

5. The Research Department therefore hurriedly prepared a new document for the NEC — to provide the basis for a Manifesto which reflected the position of the Party, and which included the agreements *already* reached in the NEC-Cabinet Group ("Manifesto 1979: the main policy proposals"). This document, RE: 2138, was made available to the NEC at the special meeting on the Monday morning, April 2.

But at this meeting the contents of RE: 2138 were not discussed at all. It was agreed only to establish a drafting committee, consisting of the Chairman and Vice-Chairman; the Chairmen of the Home Policy and Organisation Committees; the Leader and Deputy Leader; a Trade Unionist; and the General Secretary. But no remit whatever was given, on policy issues, to the drafting committee. It was merely instructed to work on the basis of RE: 2138 (which it did not do) and to make it considerably shorter (which it certainly did).*

*The document presented to the NEC (RE: 2138) was about 12,500 words in length. The final Manifesto, excluding the long introduction by the Prime Minister, was about 8,500.

Fifth stage: the Drafting Committee

The Drafting Committee met on the same day as the NEC (April 2), in the early evening, at No.10 Downing Street. It went on to about 3.30am the next day:

1. The No.10 draft was circulated to members of the Committee shortly before the beginning of the meeting and time set aside for members to read it. (This was the first time the NEC members of the Committee had seen the draft.)

2. Within a very short space of time, the No.10 draft became, in effect, the basis for discussion. If NEC members wished to include items from their own document (RE: 2138) then they had to move additions.

3. This quickly became rather difficult. First, because the Committee had agreed at the outset that it wanted a short document (which inevitably meant chopping out policy). Second, because the Prime Minister had insisted that the number of commitments be strictly limited, even when the resource cost was tiny or where there was little disagreement in substance. Instead of filling the Manifesto with such commitments, he argued, the NEC should approach the appropriate Ministers *after* the election to agree what should be done; and he, the Prime Minister, would ensure that progress was made.

4. It also became apparent that in the absence of the respective Chairmen of the various NEC sub-committees — *and* of the interested Ministers —

some items of policy would receive less than a fair hearing. (Of necessity, NEC members have to specialise, as do Ministers.)

5. NEC members became fully aware only at this meeting about the degree of hostility within the Cabinet to certain commitments. (This even included such items as Civil Service reform, on which little significant opposition had been registered either at Conference, in the NEC-Cabinet Working Group on the Machinery of Government, or in the NEC-Cabinet Group on the Manifesto). In the end, on such diverse issues as targets for unemployment, the Lords, public ownership (construction, the NEB, BP, agricultural land, plant manufacturing, etc.), local authority mortgage lending, planning, or freedom of information, the items had either to be dropped altogether or a meaningless sentence or so included. In part this was because most members of the Committee felt that as little as possible should be left "in square brackets" (i.e. not agreed) for the full NEC-Cabinet meeting to determine.

By the end of the first long meeting of the Drafting Committee the NEC members had been able to considerably improve the No.10 draft. The Committee met again on the morning of *Wednesday, April 4* to consider the revised draft — but only minor changes were agreed. It was then left to the No.10 staff, together with the Research and International Secretaries, to polish up the draft for the Friday meeting. Eventually, only three major issues had to be left in "square brackets": on the statutory powers needed to support the system of planning agreements; on construction; and on the House of Lords.

Final stage: The Clause V meeting

On Friday, April 6 at 10.00am, NEC members (apart from the handful on the Drafting Committee) had their first opportunity to see the draft Manifesto. Meanwhile a Press Conference had already been arranged for that evening, to launch the Manifesto; Labour's official campaign had been set to commence on the following Monday; and our candidates had been told that the copies of the Manifesto would be on their way by the weekend. (Ironically, the Tories were not due to publish *their* Manifesto until the following Wednesday). Thus, despite all the planning over the previous two years, all the meetings, all the decisions, the NEC had been set-up to agree the very kind of Manifesto, in the very circumstances it had always hoped to avoid.

A considerable number of useful amendments, however, were made to the draft — although on two of the three contentious issues referred to by the meeting from the Drafting Committee there was precious little success for the NEC: that on the statutory powers needed to back planning agreements, for example, was resolved by re-affirming the inadequate text set out previously in the 1974 Manifesto; that on the Lords, by watering down the abolition commitment to one promising simply to end their powers of delay.

On construction there *was* some movement — with agreement on a paragraph which, though extremely unclear, could have been exploited, had we won the election, by a Minister keen to implement Party policy.

What Went Wrong?

All in all, however, the Manifesto which emerged was remarkably weak in terms of Party policy — weaker even, on certain key issues, than the tripartite statement "Into the Eighties", to which the Government itself had been a party. It may be helpful for us to consider briefly some of the reasons why this was so — and some of the lessons for the future:

1. At the heart of the problem of agreeing the Manifesto lay the unwillingness of the Labour Government to concede to the Party any real measure of joint determination or joint control in terms of policy or strategy. This, indeed, is the real key to the problem. It meant that, by the time we began our serious work on the Manifesto, the course of the Government had been solidly set. And it was a very different course to that wanted by the Party. The Government, indeed, had become accustomed to going its own way: it was almost impossible for it to change tack just for the Manifesto.

   This factor was especially important in draft- the critical economic and industrial sections of the Manifesto — the real core of Labour's programme for the future. The differences in approach between the two sides had become impossible to bridge through the medium of the Manifesto alone, or through NEC-Cabinet Working Groups. This explains, for example, why there was no commitment to halve unemployment within the lifetime of the new Parliament; why there was no clear commitment on expanding public ownership into manufacturing; why there was no mention at all about the multinational corporations; or why there was nothing whatever of substance on the banks and financial institutions.

It was, perhaps, wishful thinking on our part to believe that the Government would jointly agree, for the current Parliament, policies it had rejected in the past. And the Government did have a point. For when a political Party is in office, the Manifesto *has* to be seen as a development from the existing policies of the Government, not the signal for a sudden lurch towards a completely new strategy.

The real lesson is that the NEC and the Parliamentary leadership must learn to work together — to *jointly* determine policy and strategy, whether in or out of office. For unless they do so, the preparation of the Manifesto will become something of an empty procedural exercise. The starting point, it is suggested, could be the establishment of a standing joint committee (of Party officers, Committee Chairmen, and members of the Parliamentary Committee) which would meet at least monthly to iron out differences *as they arise.*

THE MANIFESTO

2. Notwithstanding better working arrangements between the NEC and the Parliamentary leadership, the latter must in future be expected to come clean, at Conference and elsewhere, on its opposition to Party policy — and seek to resolve such differences, through joint agreement, with the NEC. For it is surely quite wrong for the Party to be encouraged to adopt, almost without dissent, major planks of policy (as it did on the House of Lords) and then, at the very last fence, to be faced with a complete veto on its inclusion in the Manifesto. This again indicates the need for continuing arrangements for the joint determination of policy and strategy.

3. The NEC needs also to give serious consideration again to the *nature* of the Manifesto. Is the Manifesto to be seen as the main vehicle for our election propaganda? Or should it be, as the Home Policy Committee appeared to want, "a programme of action, clear and unambiguous, for the next Labour Government"? As it turned out, commitment after commitment was dropped from the Manifesto draft for no other reason than to save words — and with little or no regard for overall priorities*

*The office should perhaps take its fair share of the blame for the way in which the No.10 draft was foisted on the NEC. We could have, after all, prepared our own version of a 7,000 word Manifesto. But this would have meant Transport House officials taking it upon themselves not only to chop to pieces the agreements reached in the NEC-Cabinet Group but also to drop numerous important Party policy commitments. The NEC rightly gave us no authority to carry out this part of surgery: but perhaps we should have done it anyway.

It was noticeable during the election that spokesmen were often called upon to "fill out" some of the vague phrases contained in the Manifesto. On the key issue of prices, for example, the very details of stronger controls contained in the original NEC draft (and dropped from the No.10 draft) later had to be spelt out by Roy Hattersley at a special Press Conference — because no one, otherwise, could be sure what we meant. It may be sensible in the future, therefore, for the NEC and Cabinet to agree not one, but two documents: a short, sharp Manifesto digest of say 5000 words or so, for wide distribution among the general public (which would also set out the main themes of the campaign); and a rather longer document, of 12-15,000 words, giving the details of the commitments we hope to fulfill during the next Parliament. It may then be possible to indicate a good deal more clearly both the *priorities* and the *costs* involved in the five year programme we are presenting to the electorate. And it would help to ensure our own accountability to both the electorate and to the Party.

4. Even with such a 'two-tier' arrangement, we can assume that there will again be a need in the future to establish a joint Drafting Committee during the final stages of preparation. The mistake this time round, surely, was not the establishment of a Drafting Committee but the

failure to provide it with a clear remit on which commitments were to be included and which could be dropped.

The lack of guidance from the NEC did help to weaken the NEC input on the Drafting Committee. In some cases for example, not all the NEC members present had detailed knowledge of the thinking behind certain long-standing NEC commitments, and thus could not always be sure of the significance of accepting a particular form of words (taxation, agriculture, price controls and the NHS are examples here).*

Even more serious, NEC members on the Drafting Committee were, at times, either not particularly sympathetic or committed to the NEC position or were actually hostile (as, for example, on child benefits being raised to the same level as the short-term NI child dependancy rate). This did not make for easy drafting.

5. But perhaps most important of all, the NEC and the Parliamentary Leadership must agree next time to publish and publicise their Manifesto proposals well in advance of any election campaign. This, indeed, was a major weakness in the Manifesto arrangements: we failed to give ourselves sufficient time to get over to the electorate what our programme was about; and

*Transport House officials, of course, have this kind of information to hand. But they cannot be expected to carry the necessary political clout during this kind of exercise. (The Research Secretary was in fact gently asked by the Prime Minister to stop raising so many objections.)

we so boxed ourselves in to Press deadlines that there was no possibility of proper consideration being given to the draft. The answer, of course, is to publish a jointly agreed Campaign Document well before an election is likely to be called (possibly presenting it also to Conference for endorsement); and then to use this Campaign Document as the basic text for the actual Manifesto discussions when they begin.

XI

Capital, Labour and the State

Stuart Holland, MP

It is arguable that Labour since 1974 has managed British capitalism in a manner which would have been inconceivable for British Conservatism of either the Heath or Thatcher variety. Labour represents the Left of Centre of the mainstream political spectrum in Britain, and to this extent justified the epithet left-wing. Yet it has implemented policies in government which have involved major cuts in projected public expenditure, wage restraint imposed by an offer which the unions felt they could not refuse without restoring Conservative government, subservience to the IMF, massive public subsidy of the private sector and a total failure to mobilise the power of business in the so-called industrial strategy for the regeneration of British industry. Its policies have failed to restrain an increase in unemployment of nearly a million to levels inconceivable by the consensus majority during the heyday of Keynesian politics. Its expenditure cuts have threatened the welfare state framework established as the main achievement of the post-war Labour government.

In short, Labour has pursued policies of a kind

which appear to confirm its incapacity to change or transform capitalism in Britain. Its 'left wing capitalism' appears a thoroughly familiar, but outdated disorder. Compared with the period 1945-51, when Labour did achieve a fundamental and until now unreversed change in the balance of power in favour of working people and their families, the periods of Labour government since 1964 have left no major record of radical policies or irreversible advance. Indeed, the new Conservatives, under leadership from the most reactionary fraction of their Party and class, managed to appear radical to much the electorate in May 1979.

What Went Wrong?

One reason lies in the attempt of Labour in government to occupy the middle ground of politics and appeal to the floating voter. But this commonplace is not enough to understand the nature of the government's divorce from Party and TUC policy, nor the reasons why the so-called middle ground did not support Labour in strength and reject the New Toryism. Some argue that the electorate have got what they voted for, with VAT increases offsetting reductions in personal income tax, a massive switch of real income and wealth to the rich and super-rich, and an attack on public spending and the welfare State which Labour would not have introduced. But the plain fact remains that the edge of Thatcher's axe was not only ground in the Treasury under a Labour administration, but fell and fell again in successive

Labour budgets. The monetarism blue in tooth and claw, which we now see ardently advocated from government benches, was adopted against Party opinion by Labour ministers in the Treasury and Cabinet. In practice, Labour voters could well have wondered which Twin was the authentic Tory.

Even in the debates and public statements which have followed the Conservative election victory, we have seen leading spokesmen of the Party assume Tory terms of reference in their attack on the first budget from the new government. Some have satisfied themselves by disputing whether wages and public spending under the last months of Labour's administration were too high, rather than challenging the principle that wages and public spending are themselves inflationary. Individual spokesmen have actually published articles saying that we should be blunt about the record and admit that Labour's previous commitment to full employment and high public spending now is unfeasible, and should be formally abandoned.

One irony in this situation lies in what we are being asked to abandon. This is less commitment to the kind of radical and socialist policies formulated in the early 1970s, and endorsed by successive conferences, than the form of social democracy which we have been assured, for some twenty years, was the practical alternative to more fundamental change. It is not that the 1974 to 1979 government tried Labour Party policies and found they failed, but that they failed to try those policies in the first place. What has failed has been not socialism, but the pragmatic social democracy of the model associated with Hugh Gaitskell and his generation. This was itself shown in Anthony Crosland's efforts in Cabinet to oppose the savagery of the IMF terms, when he found to his surprise that those he had previously considered natural allies had abandoned commitment to high public spending and equality in favour of their new 'realism' of rolling back the frontiers of the welfare state to make room for private profit.

How do we explain such factors, to ourselves and within the Labour movement? Crucially, how do we relate any insights we may gain to campaigning politics in opposition? Further, how do we try to make sure that the Labour Party does not simply stay 'left wing' capitalist versus the 'right wing' capitalism of the current government? Besides which, how can we relate analysis of what went wrong to what is to be done if Labour is to face not only the next few years, but also a period of future government as a credible radical force?

It is said by some both in and outside of the Labour Party that Labour is weak on theory. It is more commonly said by others that there is too much theory and too little organisation within the Party. In fact, certainly for a decade, the analysis of capitalist power and the need for radical policies has been strongly put by many in the movement, and reflected in detailed Party policies. Such theory may appear abstract to some, or irrelevant to others. But without a framework of analysis of what went wrong, too many of our judgements tend to be personalised or superficial — focusing for instance on who is leader of the Party, with

CAPITAL, LABOUR AND THE STATE

what team, rather than why they reject socialist policies, and on what terms.

The following argument is offered as a contribution to what must be an on-going debate within the Labour Party and movement. It is at points abstract and diagrammatic, but unashamedly so. For abstraction is crucial to generalisation. Also, while diagrams in one sense simplify the complexity of power relations in society, they also can highlight the reasons for divorce between principles and practice in recent Labour history. They are not a complete guide to events, or explanation of failures, but they may contribute insights of some use in not only a *post-mortem* but also regeneration in the movement in a period of opposition politics.

The framework of this analysis identifies five main power factors in our society. These are respectively:

1. Politics, including political parties in particular, but also the political process as engaged in by pressure groups of various interests, and non-parliamentary bodies;

2. The State, meaning not only government through politicians, forming a cabinet and various more junior posts, but also local authorities, and the central and local civil service, plus the judiciary, and the instruments of force and enforcement, i.e. the army and police;

3. Ideology, incorporating not only the limited arena of ideas as such, but also the wider framework of values, assumptions, presumptions, presuppositions and plain prejudice in terms of which

actions are influenced and implicitly 'legitimated' by various groups with society;

4. Capital as both a factor of production and a social force, with specific relations between big and small business, multinational and national enterprise, and managers and managed;

5. Labour as a factor of production and social force in a similar sense, including big and small unions, unionised and non-unionised labour etc.

Such categories in the distribution of power are not mutually exclusive. Clearly both capital and labour have direct representation in politics and government through the Conservative and Labour parties, and respective front benches. As clearly. anyone can have not only explicit ideas on politics, the economy and society, but also implicit assumptions on what is legitimate or illegitimate for government, management and unions. In particular, the press and media both reinforce such perceptions, and in part create them, thus reinforcing and reproducing a collective attitude towards politics and economics in society.*

Some analysists have sought to explain the power relations in a capitalist society by a simple division of such factors as outlined above into a two category model — meaning by model an abstraction or simulation of how such power works in practice in the system. Thus they have distinguished essentially between the economic

---

*I have already elaborated a specific analysis of the role and power on the press, on similar lines to those applied here in a wider context, in *Countervailing Press Power*, in James Curran (ed) *The British Press: A Manifesto*, Acton Society and Macmillan, 1978.

base or *sub*-structure of the system and its political, governmental and ideological *super*-structure.

For instance, a conventional analysis of super-structure and sub-structure could be represented diagrammatically as follows:

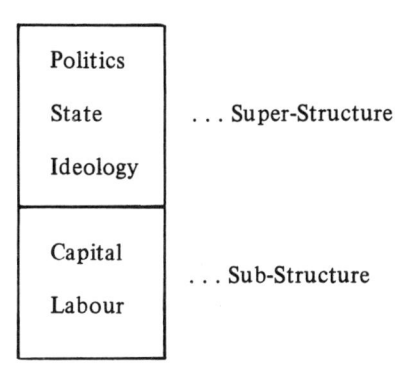

Politics / State / Ideology	... Super-Structure
Capital / Labour	... Sub-Structure

Broadly, in such a 'model' of the system, what happens in the economics of the base determines what happens in the super-structure of thought and political action. Such reasoning is implicitly deterministic, rigid, mechanical, and wide open to the parody which Edward Thompson has recently lavished on it.*

But it is highly arguable that Thompson has over-reacted to abuse of such models by throwing out base and superstructure with their determinist bathwater. The complexity of the real world is more immediately taken into account by recognising that ideas and ideology are not simply a reflection of what happens in the basic relations between

*E.P. Thompson, *The Poverty of Theory*, Merlin Press, London, 1978.

capital and labour, but constitute what amounts to an intermediary role between them. Also a re-arranged relationship between the five main factors as follows makes more sense by distinguishing an essentially *institutional* super-structure from an economic sub-structure or base.

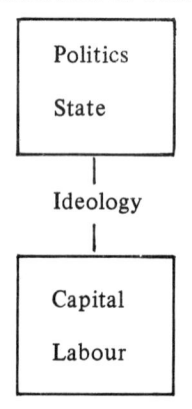

```
┌─────────────┐
│   Politics  │
│    State    │
└─────────────┘
       │
    Ideology
       │
┌─────────────┐
│   Capital   │
│   Labour    │
└─────────────┘
```

In practice, such structures do not operate in a vacuum. They function within a matrix or womb of class relations and civil society itself. In other words, class relations do not simply happen between capital and labour at the workplace or in production, distribution and exchange, as otherwise implied by the concept of economic base. Nor are they simply 'reflected' in the politics of class or class struggle at the institutional super-structure. For class background, education, the press, media and culture in a wider sense affect the ideas and ideology of those in civil society, as well as the economic base and the super-structure of political and state institutions. Conceptually, this can be viewed in the following way:

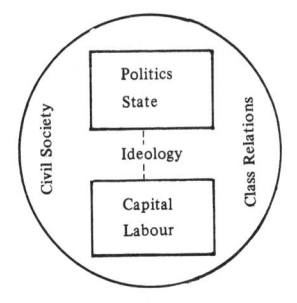

```
        ┌─────────────┐
       /│   Politics  │\
      / │   State     │ \
     /  │             │  \
Civil   ├─────────────┤   Class
Society │  Ideology   │   Relations
     \  ├─────────────┤  /
      \ │   Capital   │ /
       \│   Labour    │/
        └─────────────┘
```

How does this help explain specific phenomena and events? In fact, if we want to provide a rationale for the manner in which working class people have recently voted, on a major scale, for a Tory government which blatantly does not represent their interests, or the manner in which a Labour government has failed in practice to represent the interests of working people and trades unions, we are reasoning in terms of contradictions between what a Conservative or Labour Party says it will do — in opposition — and what it actually does in government. We also need to reason in terms of subjective perception of the role of either main Party in the system, and who objectively dominates the system as a whole, in whose interests.

In practice this amounts to using the concepts of contradiction and dominance, and relating them to the main power factors in British society today.

For instance, the dominant ideology in Britain remains one of liberal capitalist politics and economics. Within such a framework it is assumed that the political institutions of parliament and local councils control the State institutions both centrally and locally: i.e. the government and civil service and the local authorities. Similarly, it is assumed that State institutions, subject to the democratic political process, can control the employment and distribution of capital and labour in the economic sub-structure.

But there are key contradictions between the perceptions of conventional wisdom — such as a 'sovereign' parliament or 'dominant' trades unions — and the realities of political and economic power. In practice, State institutions — government, civil service in particular — dominate the decision-making process in the super-structure, while capital dominates the allocation of resources at the sub-structural level. In reality, both the political process and labour tend to be marginalised within the system, which is concentrated on the State and capital, and serviced by the dominant ideology. Diagrammatically, this can be represented as follows:

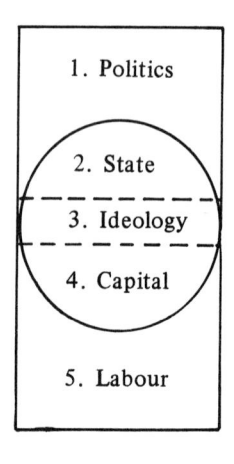

1. Politics
2. State
3. Ideology
4. Capital
5. Labour

CAPITAL, LABOUR AND THE STATE

Within this framework, the dominant ideology need not *directly* serve the system, as a capitalist mode of politics or production, but may service it *indirectly* by giving a false or contradictory account of real events.

For example, if one specifies the characteristics of the dominant fraction or section of capital, at level 4, it includes the following:

Dominant ...	Monopoly	Multinational	Producer Sovereignty
Dominated ...	Competition	National	Consumer Sovereignty

Inversely, if one specifies the characteristics of the dominant economic ideology, at level 3, it includes the following:

Dominant ...	Competition	National	Consumer Sovereignty
Dominated ...	Monopoly	Multinational	Producer Sovereignty

This is witn a definition of monopoly relating to both size and price-making power: it does not mean wholly collusive practices.

In other words, the ideology and the dominant form of production, distribution and exchange (or sub-mode within capitalism as a whole) are contradictory. The contradiction has two major results: (1) it masks the direct inter-relation between big business and the State, and (2) undermines liberal capitalist policies at the State level which are based on an outdated assumption of national firms engaged in a price competitive struggle against the rest of the world economy.

Again, the prevailing ideology assumes that capital and labour are equal in their relations with the State. The illusion is reinforced by the relative balance at the political level between the links of the Conservatives with the CBI and the links of the Labour Party with the unions. In pluralist theory, this is represented as a basic equality, with organised labour, in the form of the trades unions 'countervailing' organised capital, i.e.

Capital ⟵⟶ Labour

while in fact the relationship is in key senses one of dominance of capital over labour, or

Capital
↓↑
Labour

with only limited reactive power of labour to initiatives taken by capital.

The dominance can be illustrated by considering the range of decisions on which capital, rather, takes the initiative in the disposal of resources. In practice this amounts to what shall be produced, why, when, where, for whom, by whom, how, and costing how much. Translated into economic factors, it means the following:

1. What . . . Type of product or service (genuinely new or revamped);
2. Why . . . Private profit;
3. When . . . Timing of investment (rarely during recession);
4. Where . . . Location (whether home or abroad, and in what urban area or region);
5. To whom . . . Market (domestic or foreign, intra-company transaction or not);
6. By whom . . . Labour (at home or abroad, male or female, skill level in which country, etc.);
7. How . . . Capital-labour ratios, technology and the work process;
8. How much . . . Wages and production cost.

The limited reactive capacity of labour is illustrated by the fact that the conventional trades union bargaining role over wages and working conditions covers only two of the eight factors, and even then only marginally the 'how' factor, i.e. capital-labour ratios, technology and control over the work process. Put differently, Ford workers may with reason cite the fact that they control the speed of the line at Dagenham, but mass assembly production of private cars is determined by the management.

The main union role is focused on 'how much'. And here, most importantly, multinational companies can substantially determine 'how much' through their control of the ratio of capital to labour (and thus productivity potential) as well as by manipulation of transfer prices in trade between subsidiaries in such a way as to declare profits which are lower than real profits, thus reducing the bargaining power of labour even in its main reactive or defensive role. The initiative over all the factors remains with capital, and its power both to propose and dispose of resources.

The analysis has major implications for the question of a return to 'free collective bargaining' by the trades unions. When the decisions on what, why, when, where, to whom, by whom and how have been taken by management on a unilateral basis, it is arguable that 'free' bargaining on 'how much' is similar to a 'free offer' concession on products to consumers. The primary, active and central power over the disposal of resources stays with capital. It may well concede more to labour than it otherwise would wish, through free collective bargaining. But in general, big business can determine the whole framework of reference for conventional collective bargaining on wages.

In other words, even at the sub-structure of the system, trades union bargaining is marginalised under present conditions. When governments then introduce pay policies, whether statutory, so-called voluntary, or of the godfather variety — making offers which the unions cannot afford to refuse — the weight of the central power structure of the system (State, Ideology and Capital) is thrown against an already marginalised labour movement.

This clearly has two major implications within the wider movement: for trades unionists themselves, on the one hand, and politicians and ministers on the other. Faced with the simple arithmetic of wage increases in relation to productivity gains, many trades union leaders and many ministers and back bench members, tend to accept the logic of an incomes policy irrespective of the real imbalance of power between labour and capital. Thus many of them support policies for 8 per cent or 5 per cent wage limits partly because they view union power and wage increases as central to the inflation syndrome, and partly because they accept false reasoning on production costs, rather than investment, export structure and demand as crucial to the nation's economic problem. Although the realities of the situation indicate that unions need to move beyond the wage bargain and into decision making within big business, and government, as a condition for adequately defending wages themselves over the long run, too many trades unions leaders between 1975 and 1978 pulled their punches on such demands and put their weight behind wage restraint.

In a similar way, too many ministers saw 'no alternative' to wage restraint and — ultimately — a 5 per cent wage limit — in response to the economic crisis of the mid and later 1970s. Some had not accepted the Labour Party case for a new economic strategy when it was first formulated and endorsed by Conference in the period 1972-73 — not least the Wilson attempt at a 'veto' on the argument of the Opposition Green Paper on The National Enterprise Board, which maintained that without a controlling public stake in from 20 to 25 of the top 100 companies in the system, there would be no direct capacity to push through change in the economy and pull related change through Planning Agreements. Labour's Programme 1973 and the 1974 manifestos had specified that decisions on the allocation of resources by dominant business in both the state and private sector should be jointly negotiated by government, unions and management through the Planning Agreements procedure. In this way, Planning Agreements as a process of social negotiation were supposed to open the feasibility of change in the planning criteria of the economic and social system as a whole. The domination of private criteria should be reversed to establish a dominance of public and social criteria in the use of resources. Similarly, the domination of private control should be reversed for the establishment of social control.

The political endorsement of such a strategy by the Party Conference was a necessary condition for its fulfilment in practice in government. But it was not a sufficient condition, substantially because of the contradiction between the liberal theory of the State and the reality of capitalist State power. For instance, according to the theory — with its reflection in the prevailing ideology or 'conventional wisdom' — government is accountable to parliament, the civil service to government, and private power to public power. In terms of 'dominance', this amounts to the following schema:

Dominant	...	Parliament	Government	Public Authority
Dominated	...	Government	Civil Service	Private Authority

But in practice, the situation tends to be the

CAPITAL, LABOUR AND THE STATE

reverse, i.e.

Dominant	...	Government	Civil Service	Private Authority
Dominated	...	Parliament	Government	Public Authority

Put differently, the perceived situation, in the conventional wisdom, is one in which parliament should be able to exert a dominant influence on government, and government on the civil service, in the following manner:

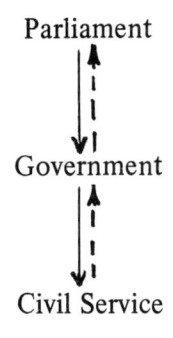

Parliament
↕
Government
↕
Civil Service

The 'feedback' mechanism in such a diagrammatic representation is supposed to represent administrative constraints (from government to parliament) and executive or technical constraints (from the civil service to government).

But in reality, the situation tends to be the reverse, at least under social democratic, Labour governments, with a sequence closer to the following:

Civil Service
↕
Government
↕
Parliament

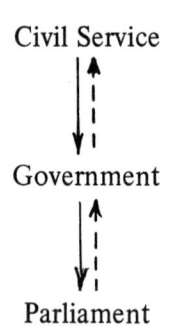

It is important to stress that such a sequence is not simply a matter of civil service conspiracy against the policies of an elected Party. Moreover, it is possible that such a sequence can be reversed if a government comes to office determined to wield power in favour of the class it represents, and is backed by a sufficient political base to exert what amounts to a hegemonic position.

But the periods in which politics really has dominated over government and the State have been exceptional. Arguably 1945 to 1951, or more strictly 1945 to 1948/9 was such a period, depending on the economic background of slump in the 1930s, the appeasement of fascism by the Tories, and their relative unreadiness for war, plus the increased radicalism within Labour Party politics which was not only a reaction to both slump and appeasement, but also to MacDonald's coalition government. Even the 1945 Labour government, despite major advances in health and other public services, and in beginning the end of formal imperialism, was as reluctant to change key aspects of the distribution of power in society – or detach itself from colonial wars in areas such as Malaysia — as some of its predecessors and successors have been.

In fact, it is important to bear in mind that much of the success of that government depended centrally on a new prevailing ideology not of socialism, in the Labour Party, but of progressive, liberal welfare statism within the power centres of the system. Keynes and Beveridge — both closer to the Liberal Party than to Labour — were the touchstones of the period, rather than socialism or Clause IV. Even those industries and services which Labour brought into public ownership at the time were nationalised with relative impunity by governments of Left coalitions, Right or Centre in the same period, in France and Italy. The structural distribution of public ownership in Western Europe as a whole shows little variation overall from that in Britain then or now.

Similarly, it is important to recognise that the counter challenge to Labour's new policies in the 1970s was mounted by the press, City of London and CBI on reactionary grounds. But the battle against such policies was mobilised and won — within government — not simply on the extreme ground occupied by such cohorts of capital, but by leading civil servants *and ministers,* many of whom rightly saw the new policies for the extension of new public ownership, planning powers over big business, and shopfloor democracy as different from the Keynes-Beveridge synthesis of liberal capitalism or social democracy on which they had been weaned as junior officials or junior ministers in the 1940s.

Not least, their own prevailing ideology or overview of 'legitimate' government, assumed that it was they who should bring government from Whitehall to working people, rather than people themselves who should formulate and bring their own demands to Whitehall. Also, within industry, they sought to preserve management's 'freedom to manage' without distinguishing technical from strategic decision making, or allowing a real say for working people in management of their own concerns. In short, they sought to preserve a framework of unreconstructed class relations in society, with themselves as the ruling elite.

Such determination to preserve the *status quo*, despite the patent crisis of Keynesian welfare statism, assumed at times the character of a virtual crusade against Labour Party and TUC policy. In other respects, it was shown in the form of increasing contempt for ideas and action which — from Conference and the CLPs — challenged the right of the 'leadership' to determine what the movement could have, when, how and on whose terms. Besides, since the Keynesianism of the post-war period was so shallowly based — less on Keynes' own emphasis on the need for controls and more on his anticipation of 'compromises and devices' by which the State would relate to business — the Keynesian brigades were decimated by the monetarist virus in government. The combination of recession and inflation, which had not occurred in the more price competitive capitalism of Keynes' own time, swept them off their feet, while their own ideological and psychological distance from Party thinking and policy left them isolated from the body of thought, support and action which could have helped defend the fabric of public spending, fuller employment and the welfare state.

Such central — ideological — factors both legitimated and reinforced the defence of government dominance of the political process in parliament. For one thing, many Labour back benchers — often in contrast with their constituency parties — shared the government's view that there was no realistic alternative to wage restraint and public spending cuts. Others were anguished by the cuts, and saw elements of the case for a radical alternative strategy. Yet they felt unable to challenge the new direction of government policy following the IMF terms, despite the fact that they had not been fully consulted on the change of direction, and despite the blatant manner in which some ministers embraced the IMF as an alibi for the wage restraint and public spending cuts to which they were already committed.

In practice, having rejected Party policy and Conference decisions, and thus the voice of the Party outside parliament, the government sought to isolate opposition from its own back benchers by offering a formula of extended patronage to some and the threat of a Tory government to others. With a few notable exceptions such as the Rooker-Wise amendment, it succeeded. But thereby it clearly moved to a period of administration of the system, rather than the pursuit of even those radical measures, such as a Freedom of Information

Act, on which it could have gained Liberal or other support.

The rationale for this new phase of administration, with the leadership isolated from the wider movement as a whole, appeared very clearly in the then Prime Minister's address to the nation in the Autumn of 1978 explaining why he, after consulting with the Queen and the Cabinet, rather than also the government and the Party, had taken his decision not to go to the country. Essentially his message amounted to saying that the country in general, and business confidence in particular would only suffer from the chopping and changing of policies which an election would represent. The same argument has of course been used in other countries as a case against elections in general. In the particular British case, it was a rationale for administration *rather than* government. Such a case would have delivered the government into the hands of the civil service, if it had not already been handed down by the civil service in the first place.

Such a contempt for the economic and social policies of the movement, and such regard for the views of so-called neutral officials, cannot be seen simply in terms of the structures of decision-making, important though they are. The legitimation of such a divorce between Party and government stemmed from the wider ideological factors already outlined, which themselves derived from a basic framework of values held by many of the post-war generation. In one form, this assumed that Britain was already over-governed, that public spending had reached its upper limits, that initiative crucial to a free society was being restrained, and that the case for relative 'dis-engagement' of government was already established. In a more basic form, such reasoning, or implicit assumption, coincided with much of the rationale for government dis-engagement which we have since heard given from Tory ideologues such as Sir Keith Joseph or Michael Heseltine. Many who have never read either Milton Friedman or Friedrich von Hayek echo their view that 'more government' will lead to loss of personal freedom and take us further down a road to serfdom.

In the parody form propagated by the leaders of *The Sun, The Mail, The Daily Telegraph* and the past *Times*, such a rationale amounted to a smear campaign that there is but a banana skin between 'Bennery' and Bolshevism. But while these wider factors are important, there also are internal structures of power and decision-making within the civil service which place governments in their hands unless backed by a powerful counter ideology, and political pressure on a major scale through democratic Party politics. Put simply, the conventional wisdom is right enough in maintaining that government today is more complex than when Gladstone, with a dozen administrators, could run the Home Office. Thereby governments, like Gulliver, can find themselves bound by myriad threads, even in those situations when the civil service is not actively forming a 'Whitehall view' different from that of the Party in government, and aiming to tie the government to the middle ground by stronger bonds.

Such bondage of government to the civil service, as already argued, may well be suppliant and willing. Masoch, as much as Marx, might be recommended reading for students of modern politics. But irrespective of whether some ministers actually enjoy their role as 'reasonable' defenders of a crisis ridden *status quo* — the bulk of the activity of any minister in government depends on some kind of support from within the civil service. As and until this is changed by political pressure for more open government, for an accountable leadership, including election and re-selection of the Cabinet, the hiring and firing of civil servants from senior posts — by ministers rather than the Prime Minister — and the creation of more politicised counter forces to the civil service in government, the 'Whitehall view' will tend to prevail against appointed and unradical ministers.

Active civil service opposition to radical government initiatives thus may be blocked by sufficient political force from governments of either the Right or Left. But its forms are extensive and, ultimately, insidious. While the Prime Minister may determine the form of Cabinet sub-committees in the manner well described by Richard Crosman — excluding strong ministers for the main part, and ensuring that the majority think with him rather than for themselves or with the Party — civil servants literally service such committees and restrict their terms of reference through parallel inter-departmental committees within the bureaucratic machine. Thereby they control the formulation of joint inter-departmental proposals going to Cabinet, which are reduced to the lowest common denominator acceptable to the officials of the departments concerned. The regular meetings of the heads of civil service departments, the 'permanent under-secretaries', seal such a process. This 'Whitehall' view includes the importance of preventing any radical measure which will destabilise the system, whether this takes the form of 'stopping Crossman' or quite simply blocking Labour Party policies such as put to the electorate twice in the 1974 manifestos.

What Should be Done?

It is possible that current Tory policies will result in such a slump and such social discontent as to put Labour in a position to win the next election with a decisive majority. In comparison with the vicious attack on welfare state and consensus policies by the Thatcher government, the prelude of such policies under Labour from 1976 may soon appear the Indian summer of a social democratic golden age.

But if Labour is to reap the fruits of Tory policies, rather than the whirlwind of social discontent, and if it is to transcend rather than simply reverse the current Tory counter-revolution, it will need to shape and mobilise a popular strategy which transforms the compromise and disillusion with its own recent conservatism. Moreover, it will need to do so in a manner which can as clearly be grasped by the electorate as different from current Tory policies, as those policies were viewed as different from Labour's left wing capitalism between 1974 and 1979.

At a minimum, this means not only defending but extending the radical socialist alternative to social democracy, as forwarded within the Party and the movement in the early 1970s, and embodied in Party and TUC policies since 1973. Moreover, it means doing so within a framework which clearly grasps that Labour in government will always prove reactive and defensive to the power centres and structures of a capitalist society unless it not only challenges but also reverses the dominance of private interests and private profits within the system as a whole. And this in turn means grasping the nature of current capitalism and future socialism in a manner which interrelates at least the five main factors in the distribution and exercise of power, as previously identified. It is only in such a way that the Labour movement will be able to make progress on the specific reforms on internal Party democracy and the accountability of power, on which attention today, quite rightly, is being focused.

If such a socialist alternative were implemented it would mean reversing or revolving the main axis of power in the heartland of the system. In practice this would mean establishing both the political process, and labour as a social and class interest, at the centre of the system of democratic power. In terms of a previous diagram, this would mean a new central relationship between labour and its representatives, both political and economic, in parliament and the trades unions, represented essentially as follows:

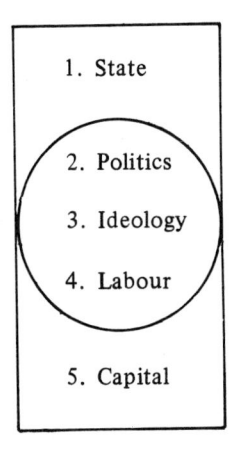

```
┌─────────────────────┐
│     1. State        │
│   ╭───────────╮     │
│   │ 2. Politics│    │
│   │ 3. Ideology│    │
│   │ 4. Labour │     │
│   ╰───────────╯     │
│     5. Capital      │
└─────────────────────┘
```

Ideology, instead of distorting and refracting the real relationships in the economy and society, would be integrated with the political process and and reflect the interests of labour in transforming the ownership and control of capital in society — effectively transforming capital itself. This implies both an active campaign by an accountable leadership for socialist policies, and also a major reform and disvestiture of the prevailing capitalist press.* Such a transformation in the power structure also would involve reversal of the at present unequal relationship between the political process, labour and the State. In other words, a transformation of State power. The form of the dominant relationship previously described would be reversed into the following:

---

*See further, Stuart Holland, *Countervailing Press Power*, in James Curran (ed), *The British Press: A Manifesto*, op.cit.

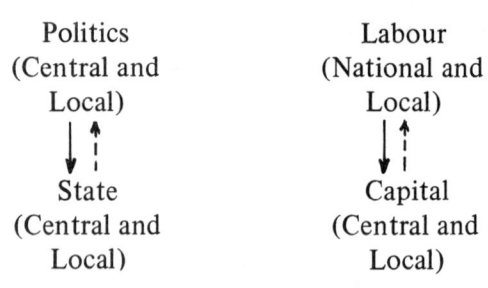

Politics (Central and Local) ↕ State (Central and Local)	Labour (National and Local) ↕ Capital (Central and Local)

In practice this would mean a situation in which the State apparatus, *qua apparatus*, would have a role in, but not dominate or rule the procedures of government. Moreover, its role itself would be more passive than active in character. In other words, officials, whether in Whitehall or Local Authorities, could have every right to argue the practicability or impracticability of a general policy or particular project. But democratisation of decision making both in government and enterprise would make feasible the dominance of the general social and public interest rather than the inconvenience or 'change in life' factor for the officials, or managers. Besides which, the questions of practicability or impracticability would be put into a general social and political context, so that the infeasibility of a particular issue within actual terms of reference could be transformed by changing the terms of reference themselves (e.g. public enterprise where private enterprise resisted a particular pressure for change, majority workers' control where conventional management — under Bullock or non-Bullock terms -- refused to implement a proposal endorsed by both government and company unions, and so forth).

In practice, dominance for the political process over the State apparatus should be acceptable either to those who are Liberal in political allegiance, or those who believe in the basic principle that governments should be accountable. In other words, such a principle should be acceptable to a wide range of the British political spectrum. The mechanisms of such accountability are secondary to the strategy for the transformation of power relationships in society, but nonetheless important in themselves. At the parliamentary level they could well involve an extension of the principle of private members' motions, or personal motions, which used to dominate in parliament before the rise of the 20th century Party system. They could certainly involve a formalisation of the principle that the government would not consider a defeat on a particular issue as a vote of confidence, and the increased acceptability of qualified support for government (whether central or local) on particular motions, i.e. support in part but not in whole, with enlarged debate for amendment on particular aspects of major bills. They also should involve an extension of the procedure of parliamentary committees beyond the lines pioneered in the 1960s under the influence of Richard Crossman, and closer to the lines of the US congressional committees. At present, for instance, there are both ridiculous anomalies and substantive limits to the powers of Commons committees – e.g. the fact that a peer may refuse to appear before a Commons committee, or that a Permanent Under-Secretary may refuse to answer particular questions put by such a committee, and ministers refuse to appear at all.

In political terms, such a dominance for the political process over the apparatus of the State clearly implies democratisation of decision-making and accountability within the Labour Party. In such a context it is crucial not only to ensure the genuine accountability of members of parliament through re-selection, but also to ensure that the Leader of the Party, and the Cabinet, are elected and re-selected by the Party as a whole.

To date, these are highly contentious issues in the Labour movement, clouded by false reasoning and caricature not only in the press but also within the Party. They might be clarified by the following arguments.

1. Accountability does not in itself mean the mandating of individual members of parliament, or a government, on all specific issues. But it does mean the power to remove from position or office those who fail to respect the general mandate on which they were both selected or elected. To take a historical analogy. When Clem Attlee came into office as Prime Minister in 1945 it apparently was found that the Party's proposals for the nationalisation of coal were undetailed and inadequate as the basis for legislation. Attlee rightly enough instructed the relevant minister to prepare more detailed proposals for the Cabinet. But he affected the pace and timing of legislation, not the principle whether or not to nationalise the mines. By 1948, however, the Attlee government was losing momentum on its election commitments of

1945, and less responsive to demands from the movement. By 1951, Attlee single-handedly decided to 'go to the country' because he and some of his team judged that the parliamentary majority of the time was too small for them to handle government without difficulty. From 1948, the movement itself should have been able to remove some of the ministers concerned, or Attlee himself, not least since they already had been exhausted by five years of wartime government before facing the strains of the post-war period. Bearing in mind that Labour hardly lost a by-election between 1945 and 1951, and that its overall vote had increased in the 1951 election, it is arguable that more internal democracy within the Party and movement would have ensured that those able to advance Labour with a second generation of post-war policies, beyond the terms of the spirit of 1945, should have been appointed to take over from the Attlee generation itself and lead Labour, with however small a majority, into the 1950s in government.

2. Accountability does not mean inhibition of all tactical freedom to adjust and accommodate to circumstances in government. Circumstances change, and with them the feasibility of progress to specific ends on the kind of timetable which might well have been considered feasible before new constraints. But there is a crucial difference between the *tactical* adjustment to events by those in government, and their abandonment of the *strategy* for government formulated by the Party and movement in either opposition or government.

The situation from the 1970s rather than the 1940s is a classic example. The failure of the 1974-79 governments was not simply a matter of their claiming the right to determine the place and scale of change, but their fundamental opposition to radical change as such. Instead of a move towards a shift in the balance of power in favour of working people and their families, those governments presided over a shift away from even social democratic policies of commitment to high public spending and full employment, thereby ensuring that the crisis which we inheritied was the occasion for an attack on the fabric of the welfare state rather than for a major advance beyond the Keynesian consensus of the post-war settlement. The use of the term industrial strategy was the main 'concession' — in a classic Orwellian double-speak — towards the philosophy and strategic demands of the Party and Conference.

3. Accountability nominally threatens the power of some unions and members of parliament over Party and government policy. But there is a key difference between *nominal* power to cast votes, and *effective* power to defend political or class interests. In voting for that Leader of the Parliamentary Party whom they thought would best represent them in succession to Harold Wilson, the Parliamentary Party thereby increased the divorce between themselves and the rest of the movement. In failing to back their voting muscle at Conference with industrial muscle to demand the pursuit of Conference decisions in government, the trades unions found themselves on a collision course with

the parliamentary leadership and the Cabinet. Thereby, with a hostile press and media, and faced with pressure from the CBI and organised capital, the unions found themselves confronted by an unholy alliance between such forces and a government largely unaccountable — even on an annual basis — to Party Conference and the wider movement. Faced with the claim that they sought to *rule* the system, they found their main *role* in seeking to defend wages and working conditions was attacked by — nominally — their own government, in office. By failing to vote in 1978 for the election of the Leader of the Party on a weighted vote or electoral college — broadly one-third trades union, one-third constituency parties and one-third members of parliament and candidates — the trades unions deprived themselves of a greater voice for those who legitimately can play a forward role in defending their own rights at work and beyond the wage bargain, i.e. the wider Labour Party. Thereby, on a collision course with the government, they were partly handicapped rather than helped by the extent to which their block vote at Conference diminished the weight of the forces in the Party which could have helped them.

4. Accountability, while not feasible in the sense that the Party and wider movement should be able to reverse each and every decision of ministers, must extend to whether those ministers continue in office when they blatantly ignore not only Conference decisions but wider feeling in the movement. In this sense, selection and re-selection of individual members of parliament and the

Leader of the Party are not sufficient conditions to prevent a divorce between policies endorsed by the movement and policies pursued against the movement in government. The failure of the trades union movement to establish elementary union rights in companies such as Grunwick or Garners is a case in point, exposing the weakness of ACAS and allowing reactionary employers to call on the enforcement of their interests and exploitation, under a Labour government, through use of the police to prevent effective picketing. In the face of such a situation, the Labour Party through Conference — preferably on the same weighted vote or electoral college principle — should be able to hire and fire not only the Leader of the Party in government, on his or her overall record, but also specific ministers.

Such factors are crucial to any strategy seeking to reverse the oligarchic dominance, in government, by a largely unaccountable elite. Such regular accountability and re-selection also are legitimised not simply by the traditions of democratic socialism, but also by gurus of social democracy such as Max Weber. Weber argued with much force that anti-authoritarian forms of government could only be ensured in modern society through procedures ensuring: (a) short terms of office; (b) liability to recall at any time; (c) rotation or re-selection; (d) a strictly defined general mandate for the conduct of representative office; (e) the obligation to submit unusual issues not foreseen to the assembly of members or committee whom they represent; (f) the rendering of account for their exercise of office to such members, and so forth.* Weighed in the balance against such criteria, the Labour Party and movement of today — in its relations with government — is undemocratic even by the standards of social democracy.

Not least, the framework of new accountability is crucial to the question whether Labour in government at any time this century can repeat or advance on the kind of shift in the balance of power achieved by the 1945 government which, in areas such as housing, health, education and social security made advances which — until this Tory government — remained effectively unreversed for several decades. In other words, without the accountability of government to parliament, and parliament to the Party, there is little chance of reversing the dominance of capital over labour in class relations and civil society.

But there also are certain strategic issues which the Labour movement both must grasp and make credible if it is not only to win elections but also win in government. In key respects these embody the reversal of the dominance of capital, profit and private criteria in the allocation of resources, and their replacement by social and public criteria and guidelines. There is no bill of goods and services drawn by individuals or groups which can reflect the needs and interests of working people themselves in a finite or closed manner. But some of the items on the following agenda have already been put, with force, by individuals or groups

*Max Weber, *The Theory of Social and Economic Organisation*, ed. Talcott Parsons, William Hodge, London, 1947, p.412.

within the Labour movement and will become increasingly imperative in the impending crisis of technological or 'micro-chip' unemployment.

It should be stressed that such issues are not forwarded irrespective of the question of social control of the environment, or policies designed to avoid waste of finite resources. Although they advocate increased production, their concern is within its distribution and social control. They do and could include the following.

1. The right to *equalised employment.* This would and should differ from the conventional post-war commitment to full employment in the sense that with the application of feasible technical progress and productivity increases, output in the productive sectors of the economy can potentially increase with decreased employment. There is little valuable in itself in some of the labour force working a basic 40 hours a week plus overtime, while there are nearly a million and a half unemployed now and the possibility of 1930s levels of unemployment not far over the horizon. At present the structural, spatial and social distribution of unemployment is highly unequal. If equalised through effective planning — conceived as a process of social negotiation focused in Planning Agreements — there is no reason in socialist principle why a basic norm of a 35 hour week — or a 35 week year — should not be achieved throughout the economy. It has already been voiced by some British and continental trades unionists.

2. The right to *equalised personal income,* including income from wealth. Such a demand

makes real economic sense in the medium-term as well as representing greater social justice. One of the underlying problems in capitalist development is the tendency to structural under-consumption, rather than the cyclical under-consumption which Keynes analysed. In other words, it arises from the saturation of demand at given levels of income distribution. Thus the professional middle class is delighted by the first or second car, first or second television, first fridge and first freezer, but does not need a dozen of each. The stimulus to consumption of both goods and especially services made possible by a major social redistribution of income would not only increase the welfare of the lower paid, but also do more for the recovery of output and employment than a hundred further cuts of public expenditure, or a thousand uncoordinated wage demands through industry.

3. The right to *increased social income*. So far the government has formalised the concept of the 'social wage', or the difference between personal income and effective income represented by social security payments, rent rebates etc. But if the technical benefits of productivity increases are to be genuinely socialised, the concept of such benefits should be extended from their present *minimalist* social-casualty basis to the more *maximalist* level of a social right. The policy could be phased to that of equalising personal income, and related to the socialisation of services for which direct payment is made at present (see below). In particular, there should be a challenge to the at present essentially capitalist based entitlement

to certain 'social income' benefits only in those cases where the individual has fulfilled certain previous payments.

4. The right to *socialised public services*. Such a right is related to the concept of social income, and amounts essentially to the principle of services which are not paid directly by the user. The principle was established with the initial framework for the National Health Service, 'free' education at certain levels, and so on. It also was evident in the early activity of some public authorities, such as electrification of remoter areas on what amounted to a subsidised basis. With the fiscal crisis of the State, and in particular its failture to cover increased public expenditure from taxation of big business, the principle has been substantially replaced by a privatisation of public services. Domestic gas and electricity users, for instance, are now charged virtually double the cost per unit of industrial users. Such principles should be reversed in favour of consumers, with not only health and education, but also broad categories of housing, heating, power supply and transport taken out of the 'cash nexus' and provided on the basis of need rather than ability to pay.

Socialisation of transport, paid indirectly by rates or other taxation, rather than directly by the user, should be related to the restricted use of private transport in central urban areas, where we should give back the environment to the people.

5. The right to a *social control of work*. In essence, this should include the right to social control of the labour process, and the re-human-

isation of work which has been routinised under mass production techniques. The productivity losses which might be incurred in some cases could certainly be offset overall by the planned use of technical progress and innovation. But there also is the complementary, vital principle of workers' control of the ends of the work process: i.e. the social use and *usefulness* of the production or service concerned. The Lucas Aerospace Shop Stewards' Alternative Corporate Plan has rightly been heralded within the Labour movement as a model in this respect. It shows the feasibility of working people within business taking the initiative in the design and prototype of products with a high use value — health equipment, safety equipment and new modes of transport. It also shows the feasibility of their formulating such proposals within the context of an overall corporate plan in the big business sector.

6. The right to *socialised planning.* Such a right relates to the concept of the social control of work within the enterprise, and in its impact on the rest of the economy. In smaller business it would involve the right to new company or co-operative production, distribution and exchange backed by funds for workers' initiative and control. In bigger business, with a significant impact on the economy as a whole, such a right should include the right by workers' representation to pressure and negotiate change in big business behaviour over the broad range of corporate behaviour, i.e. the what, where, why, whose, for whom and to whom from which unions at present are effectively excluded. The

framework for such negotiation has already been elaborated in the tri-partite Planning Agreements policy, as endorsed in successive Labour Party and TUC Conferences since 1974, yet hitherto neglected by the government. Such socialised planning would involve a major extension of public ownership into the big league firms, again on the basis of Labour Party and TUC policies. It would represent the capacity for direct intervention and leverage in the planning process as the twin arm and complement of a planning strategy.

7. The right to *open government.* By implication, the right of trades union representatives to take part in Whitehall in the negotiation of new social and economic planning of big business, would represent an opening of the State apparatus to direct pressure from and representation of labour. It thereby would make possible a divorce of the at present central relationship between big business and the State. But this centralisation of the role of labour in a democratised process of resource allocation also should involve the centralisation of the political process via new rights for parliament to challenge and countervail the at present closed process of government and the effective domination of ministers by the civil service. The Labour movement should not close its perspectives on the feasible transformation of executive power by advise and consent committees of the US type, pioneered in embryo by Crossman's strengthening of the powers of Commons committees. A radical revision of the official secrets act, with a distinction between defence and civil interests should be a

CAPITAL, LABOUR AND THE STATE

crucial part of any such fundamental reform for a change in the present imbalance between the political process, labour and the exercise of State power.

8. The right to *open press and media*. This is less utopian, in key respects, than commonly conceived on parts of the Left. Despite the identifiable bias in television reporting of the current crisis, it is not clear that such bias is explicit rather than an implicit reflection of the prevailing ideology. The Independent Television Charter's formal obligation, as with the BBC, to give reasonable expression of both sides of any case imposes more constraint on television than the at present relatively unbridled one-sidedness of a high proportion of the press. For instance, West Germany is far from a model of general freedoms, especially with regard to the constraints on expression of civil servants, including university and school teachers. But the West German legislation on the press obliges newspapers to give the right of reply in specific cases of misrepresentation, with the same page space, position, type, format and layout as the misrepresentation. With new legislation on the press, providing for the break-up and dissolution of any press enterprise controlling more than some 15 per cent of a given market and the sponsorship of journalists' and workers' co-operatives in the media such advances could help transform the present mystification and mythical 'explanations' of the social and economic crisis. Similarly, if denuded of their acceptance of direct business sponsorship, and despite the current Tory aim of giving the fourth channel to

private enterprise, the Annan proposals for an 'open' fourth television channel should be welcomed. In the same way, an obligation might be legislated for the press to publish an 'open page' or open pages policy for minority groups, subject to a reformed press council, and possibly an Open Press Authority.

Such proposals by no means exhaust the strategic demands which might be made by activists in the Labour movement. But they do represent terms of reference for a change in the balance of power from capital and the State to labour and the political process. If they are to prove effective terms of reference in Britain, henceforward, they would gain through the pressure for complementary radical demands related to the kinds of policy and instruments which have been endorsed by both the Labour Party and the TUC through the 1970s. These could include the following:

1. *Defence and extension of public expenditure.* This represents the simplest way of preserving the fabric of social services, and of assuring sufficient effective demand within the system to reverse a catastrophic slump. The cuts envisaged so far have been undertaken in a monetarist framework which aims to reduce the State intervention and release 'market forces'. But this Friedmanite dogma represents the previously described fundamental contradiction within the ideology of modern capitalism. It is based on the outdated premise of private capital as the main motor of accumulation and resource allocation, ignoring even the basic

principles of Keynes' emphasis on demand. In practice, more than 85 per cent of any public expenditure goes directly or indirectly to private enterprise, since the nationalised industries and public sector enterprise account for less than 15 per cent of gross domestic product. In their excitement at the prospect of dismantling the Welfare State and restoring a 'pure' market system, the Friedmanites in their various guises (IMF, Treasury mandarins and government ministers) will condemn capitalist Britain to its pre-Keynesian pre-Welfare State crisis of chronic under-consumption.

2. *Price controls* focused on the price leaders in the system: in practice the top 100 companies which command half of Britain's output and distribution. If reflation is advocated in combination with real price controls (rather than the marginal restraint of price increases formerly endorsed by the Price Commission), the new Gordian knot of deflation and inflation which has perplexed the Keynesians and opened the way to monetarism could be cut. One of the main reasons for the deflation-inflation syndrome is the fact that business now, as opposed to the thirties, is big enough to pass on cost increases in higher prices (through greater monopolistic concentration). As demand is cut by monetarism this increases the fixed costs per unit of output through underutilised plant and equipment, plus the fixed costs of the bank and bond borrowing to which business moved (from 'passable' equity payments and stock market finance) during the sustained years of relative expansion after the war. Some higher

commodity and component costs from imports only give the twist to this underlying structural reason for the 'new inflation'. With reflation of effective demand via restored public expenditure, business would reduce its fixed costs per unit of output through higher output.

3. *Socialised Corporate Planning* accented on the top 100 companies which command half of output and employment, and more than half of direct export trade and industrial assets. As opposed to basic reflation and basic price controls, such planning – if undertaken via the tri-partite Planning Agreements policy – could be used to change the future use of resources in society rather than simply restore the demand structures of the past. The most important demand for such planning is the most feasible: a requirement on the top 100 firms to open the books to government and unions on the forward plans of big business. The key data revealed, on investment, employment, location, export and import trade and prices – would put the headlights on the medium term prospects of the economy where the government and unions have recently worked virtually in the dark. The strategy of such planning would be focused on the strong points of the system – its genuine commanding heights – rather than the at present empty boxes of Neddy seminars and talking shops. Its method of a social process of negotiation for change in the use of resources – involving the shopfloor rather than simply the boardroom and the corridors of State power – should be contrasted both with the bankrupt notion of 'planning from

the top', which in practice has reinforced in the central liaison of capital and the State.

4. *New public enterprise* and new modes of ownership, transcending the strategic and tactical limits of present public sector intervention in the economy. This should be related to the general strategy of reflation with price controls. But there is a major case for demands for some new public enterprise intervention on specific industry lines, including areas which are crucial for the effective use of public expenditure such as construction, health products and equipment, banking and insurance, and so on. In other words, as an extension of the initial Labour Party strategy of securing a controlling public holding in 20 to 25 of the top 100 companies, there should be pressure for new public corporations in sectors at present dominated by monopoly interests. As crucially, the Labour movement should not neglect the case argued in Labour Party policy from 1973 that new public enterprise, with the existing nationalised industries, should be transformed by the new mechanisms for industrial democracy made feasible by tri-partite Planning Agreements negotiation between government, unions and management (whether that management in a transitional context remains relatively conventional or is directly elected — as it should be — by those who work in the nationalised concerns or new public enterprises).

5. *National Planning* — not as a paper document such as The National Plan of 1965, or peripheralised as in the Department of Economic Affairs, but as a central focus of new resource planning in the

economy, employing the new instruments for public enterprise and planning control outlined in Labour Party policy and in the above argument. Such planning should embrace both new ends and new means. It should involve a *rolling* five year plan for resource use, with a complementary ten year planning horizon. It would provide the main framework for the systematisation of the changed planning targets of individual big business in both the public sector (new and old) and the remaining private sector. But it also should relate such company targets to industrial and regional targets for resource use. Further, it should include the Labour Party's recommendation of a National Planning Commission responsible to a Cabinet National Planning Committee of ministers. In such a way public spending could be related to public enterprise supply and planning controls in a central politicised framework, where ministers could transcend the limits of traditional budget formulation by an inner Cabinet cabal. Further, the main planning options by industry, region and leading companies should be published annually and debated by parliament and the Party Conference.

6. *Open Fiscal Policy.* This is crucial if account is taken of the fact that — at present — the top 100 companies overall are paying virtually no effective tax, rather than declaring nominal tax in their widely published and highly superficial annual company accounts. On one measure alone — tax relief on stock appreciation, the Labour government had handed back to the private sector a sum in excess of the IMF loan on which so much

was agonised and to which so much was sacrificed. The single most important further measure of tax relief is depreciation allowances on investment, followed by the panoply of R and D write-offs and regional investment grants. (The latter, on the evidence of big business itself to the Commons Expenditure Committee, have virtually no effect on their regional location decisions). The failure of the former allowances to promote investment is self-evident empirically in the fact that private sector investment has been virtually stagnant through the 1970s. It is evident analytically from the fact that no capitalist enterprise in its right mind would undertake new investment when its present capacity is massively under-employed. The new open fiscal policy should, again, be focused on big business. None of the top 100 companies should, after a given deadline, receive State subsidy or rebate without revealing their need to the unions and the government via a Planning Agreements type procedure.

7. *Planning of Foreign Trade.* From a socialist viewpoint, this wider concept represents greater international justice than the focus of demands on import controls alone. The traditional argument against such a planning of trade has been based on the bureaucracy which it would entail and the anomalies it would involve. But while this argument had a limited force during earlier stages of capitalist development, it has virtually no force in a period in which the concentration of capital has resulted in control of 40 per cent of Britain's visible exports by only 31 companies, 50 per cent by 75 companies,

and 66 per cent by 200 firms. Similarly, transfer pricing on intra-subsidiary trade by multinationals now accounts for a considerable share of overall balance of payments figures. Up to a half of the trade of the above companies is with their own subsidiaries abroad. Thus a 10 per cent transfer pricing effect via under-stated exports and over-stated imports would represent an annual average loss to the balance of payments figures of the UK of 5 per cent — the very margin of fluctuation which causes panic on the stock exchange and panic pressure on sterling. There is a clear case for import controls in some sectors of industry, but on the basis of specific 'dumping' by particular foreign countries such as Japan, and a control of *increases* in imports. While some sectors of industry, including textiles, footwear, electrical goods and television could well be granted short-term protection, this might well be complemented by a more determined use of powers to suspend specific imports during the period in which 'dumping' allegations are investigated rather than on a simple widespread protectionist policy, which would discriminate against countries whose future social development depends on exports to economies such as Britain. The real safeguard in international trade for the British economy depends on the central question of whether or not we harness the economic power of giant enterprise — across the broad range of its activity — to social ends and social needs.

8. *International Autonomy*. This issue is both general and specific. It is general to the extent that the power of the dominant ideology of capitalist

development is embodied in the policy demands of the night visitors from the IMF or other international agencies of capitalist finance. In this respect the 'will' of British Cabinets to defend their nominal autonomy relates to their capacity to command support for an autonomous model of national development. Under recent strategies this was not even attempted. The Cabinet in 1976 submitted to IMF dictates. Under the terms of reference of the alternative strategies outlined in this paper, such national autonomy becomes feasible if sufficient pressure is exerted by the labour movement on a Labour government. Clearly the question of autonomy in international affairs is raised by the current pretensions of the EEC, and especially direct elections to the European Assembly. It is important in this context that the Labour Party should actively assert its democratic and socialist internationalism, as opposed to the pseudo-democratic and capitalist supranationalism of the present Community.

Such issues, as already stressed, are neither finite nor closed. Some already are clearly on the agenda of the Party and movement. But if we are not only to react to the election defeat, and the left-wing capitalism of Labour in government, but transform the dominance of capital and profit into the dominance of public and social interests in an effective democracy, then democratic socialism must be argued, and mobilised, with reference to a transformation of the main power relationships in contemporary capitalist society.

Capital and its class power are in part embedded in civil society through the hold of a dominant liberal capitalist ideology and the central relationship of big business and the State. An anti-monopoly programme, and a campaign exposing the contradictions between the myths of liberal capitalism and the realities of monopoly and elite power, should be central, in turn, to our own thinking and campaigning. But we also need to advance beyond such legitimate negative reaction to positive action to legitimise our own democratic socialist alternatives to present power structures and their crisis.

Not least, if we are to be credible to others, we need credibility for ourselves. We cannot afford to pull our punches in the face of the most reactionary and divisive Tory government in decades by failing to admit the manner in which the door for monetarism, and an attack on the principles of a Welfare Society, was opened by our leadership, in government, and in opposition to the policy of the Labour movement. To claim that our leadership was socialist, when in practice it offered mainly capitalism with a more human face, is little basis for an advance to democratic socialism in any genuine sense.